DARTS

SKILLS
TACTICS
TECHNIQUES

CROWOOD SPORTS GUIDES

DARTS

SKILLS

TACTICS

TECHNIQUES

Patrick Chaplin

THE CROWOOD PRESS

First published in 2015 by
The Crowood Press Ltd
Ramsbury, Marlborough
Wiltshire SN8 2HR

www.crowood.com

British Library Cataloguing-in-Publication Data
A catalogue record for this book is available from the British Library.

ISBN 978 1 78500 005 8

Frontispiece: Raymond van Barneveld, multi-World title holder. (Photo: Tip Top Pics Ltd)
Additional photo credits: pages 9, 27 and 67 – Tip Top Pics Ltd

Typeset by Jean Cussons Typesetting, Diss, Norfolk
Printed and bound in India by Replika Press Pvt Ltd

CONTENTS

ACKNOWLEDGEMENTS AND DEDICATION

Acknowledgements

The Author would like to thank the following for their help and cooperation in the production of this book: Suzan Ahmet, Chris Barrell, Bill Bell, Vince Bluck (NODOR International), Steve Brown, James Copeland, Steve Daszko, Ian Flack (WINMAU Dartboard Company Ltd.), David Gill (DG Media), John Gwynne, Scott Harrison (Nuvolux Inc.), David King (Darts501.com), Robert Pringle (Harrows Darts Technology), Chris Sargeant (Tip Top Pics Ltd.), Mick Simpson, Steve Wadsworth and Tony Wood (editor of Darts World magazine 1972-2009).

Dedication

To my wife Maureen. Through thick and thin she has adjusted to my passion for the sport of darts and supported me all the way, way beyond the call of duty. Her love drives me on. Also to my very best friend Colin Barrell, who week after week turns out on a Wednesday evening to throw a few 'arrers'; something we began more than thirty-five years ago.

IMPORTANT NOTE

Darts is an adult sport. Darts are not toys: children **must** be supervised by an adult during play.

FOREWORD by Bobby George

I have known Patrick Chaplin for a good number of years. We've even appeared together on TV a couple of times. Amongst other things, I call him the Professor because he is pretty knowledgeable about darts. (He knows nearly as much as me!)

The Professor has played for many years, more than me in fact, but mostly at a recreational level. He's never been a trophy hunter and never performed on the world stage, yet here he is with this book to teach you how to play the great sport of darts!

To be honest, I wasn't sure he could pull this off but I was wrong. He knows his stuff and has mingled with the experts (including me) over time, so a lot of good advice on how to play has been either learned along the way or simply rubbed off from us professionals.

In this book, Patrick includes everything you need to know to learn how to play, covering in detail the skills, techniques and tactics that enable you to enjoy every dart thrown.

That's the way to teach it!
Luvly jubbly!

Bobby George
George Hall
Essex

www.bobbygeorge.com

Bobby George. (Photo: Tip Top Pics Ltd)

ABOUT THE AUTHOR

Dr Patrick Chaplin has been playing darts since he was twelve years old and has written authoritatively on the history and development of the sport for many years.

He has co-authored books with three professional darts players: three-time World Professional Champion John Lowe, multi world titled Trina Gulliver MBE and twice *News of the World Individual Darts Champion* Bobby George, and his articles about the world of darts have been widely published.

Patrick was awarded a PhD in 2006 by Anglia Ruskin University, Cambridge, for his dissertation Darts in England 1900-39: A Social History, which was published in book form by Manchester University Press, 2009. The title was shortlisted for the prestigious annual Lord Aberdare Literary Prize for the best book on sports history.

Known globally as Dr Darts, Patrick also writes a monthly free online publication *Dr Darts' Newsletter* (*DDN*), which is read in more than 100 countries.

He lives in Essex with his wife Maureen and their cat Angel.

Dr Patrick Chaplin. (Photo: Moppix)

PART I

AN INTRODUCTION TO THE GAME

CHAPTER 1

HISTORY AND DEVELOPMENT

Until comparatively recently, the history of darts was, by tradition, 'lost in the mists of alehouse smoke'.

Over the best part of the last century, various assumptions were made about the sport's origins and a number of myths accumulated. These myths then fell victim to embellishment and journalistic licence, with the result that they eventually became 'fact' and distorted darts' real history. However, it has now been historically proven that darts, in some form or another, has been played in English alehouses, beerhouses, inns, taverns and public houses since at least the late fifteenth century.

The most common form of the game was called 'puff and dart', in which tiny feathered darts were blown through a wooden pipe at a circular board, which usually resembled a miniature, concentric archery target.

By the mid-nineteenth century, as the nature of English fairgrounds changed from employment and agricultural fairs to an emergent form of pure entertainment, the first wooden darts with feather flights were imported from France by showmen and, with homemade wooden targets, were introduced as a sideshow 'darts game'. As a result, darts became extremely popular. Indeed, it has been

claimed that the complex and frustrating numbering sequence featured on the dartboard of today, accepted across Britain and indeed the rest of the world as 'standard', was devised by one such showman, Brian Gamlin of Bury, Lancashire. However, my research has revealed the more likely candidate to be Leeds wireworker Thomas Buckle.

By the turn of the twentieth century, 'French darts' were being imported by the toy industry, particularly Thomas Salter Ltd, and darts became popular with children. Enthusiastic travelling salesmen sold the game to public houses along the roads within their sales areas. This created

Puff and dart being played by young boys in the late nineteenth century. (Image: Author's Darts Archive)

French wooden 'H Band' dart. (Photo: Author's Darts Archive)

demand that was complemented by the interest stimulated across England and Wales by the transient fairground communities, who left the people of the villages and towns they visited with an interest in, and even a passion for, darts.

This steady growth of darts within public houses before and immediately after World War I augured well for the future of the game and came about because brewers and licensees, having survived the onslaught of the temperance movement, found themselves faced with numerous growing or new threats from alternative leisure attractions that were taking business away from pubs. These included the dance hall, cinema and spectator sports such as football and speedway.

The drinks industry, the brewers and licensees then realized (as indeed some had done before 1914) that the playing of legal games within their premises could be a way for them to fight back. As a result, various pub games were introduced (and those already in place further encouraged) as existing pub facilities were improved or enhanced. In many cases, it was a matter of simply making space available to accommodate games, of which darts was to become by far the most popular.

Brewers and licensees created and organized inter-house darts leagues, being encouraged and urged on by in-house brewery magazines and the licensing trade press. In 1925, these elements met darts organizers in London and established the National Darts Association (NDA), its main purpose being to regularize the game. Such was darts' popularity during the 1920s that the *News of the World* Sunday newspaper introduced its own darts 'test', originally only competed for in the metropolitan area of London. This began in the 1927/28 season. In the late 1930s, it began to spread nationwide and in the early 1970s it became an international tournament.

The interwar period witnessed a boom in the popularity of darts, not only among the working classes, but also the upper classes. However, the rigid class system ensured these two groups of darts enthusiasts never met in match play. Additionally, and contrary to previously accepted wisdom, recent research has shown that many women participated in leagues during this period, with many being more than a match for the men.

During World War II, darts crossed the globe as members of the British armed forces entered various theatres of war. Darts played a great part in maintaining morale throughout those dark days; the game even being played in prisoner of war camps. Allied servicemen and women stationed in England enjoyed the camaraderie of the local pubs and many

A modern bristle dartboard. (Photo: WINMAU Dartboard Co. Ltd)

were introduced to darts there. Some, including the Americans, Canadians and those from Australasia, took the game, or at least the spirit of the game, home with them and in some cases this became the nucleus of the eventual growth of darts in their countries.

A new national darts association, the National Darts Association of Great Britain (NDAGB), was formed in 1954. The NDAGB organized numerous events across Britain and helped set up some of the first county teams and leagues. However, despite the NDAGB's endeavours, the lack of radio and television coverage meant the sport returned to the pub and dropped out of general view for nearly twenty years.

In 1973, the British Darts Organisation (BDO) was formed in London and over the next decade and a half the sport was transformed from a pub game into a national pastime (and passion). With the innovation of split-screen technology and a swarm of eager sponsors, it then

ABOVE: Scotland's Jocky Wilson, twice World Champion. (Photo: Steve Daszko)

BOTTOM LEFT: John Lowe, three times World Champion. (Photo: Tip Top Pics Ltd)

BOTTOM RIGHT: Eric Bristow, five times World Champion. (Photo: Harrows Darts)

became a rip-roaring televisual success. This, in turn, led to the creation of the first darts superstars, including Eric 'The Crafty Cockney' Bristow, John 'Old Stoneface' Lowe and John Thomas 'Jocky' Wilson, all of whom became household names and remain so even today.

Such was the power and influence of the BDO that in 1977 members of that organization were instrumental in helping coordinate setting up the World Darts Federation (WDF), a global organization for the sport of darts which, at the time of writing, boasts over sixty-five member countries. The BDO also organized the inaugural World Professional Darts Championship in 1978, which is still contested today.

However, in the early 1990s a 'split' occurred in the sport when sixteen of the top professional players, their managers and a number of representatives of the darts industry broke away from the BDO to form the World Darts Council (WDC), now the Professional Darts Corporation (PDC). The purpose of this new organization was to focus specifically on the professional game, while the BDO continued to look after the grass roots of the sport and went on running its own major events. Thus, darts players and fans are today in the envious position of having two codes playing to more or less the same rules. Both bodies organize quality tournaments throughout the year, which, especially in the case of the PDC, are screened regularly on television.

In the mid-1970s, the Sports Council calculated that more than six million people in the UK played darts at either a casual or competitive level. That equated to well over ten per cent of the population. Although this number has reduced over the subsequent four decades, the popularity of darts both as an active sport and non-participative spectator experience still runs high and pub, county and super leagues continue to flourish. In addition, darts, despite the rise of computer games, is still popular as a home recreation and, although essentially an adult sport, children can

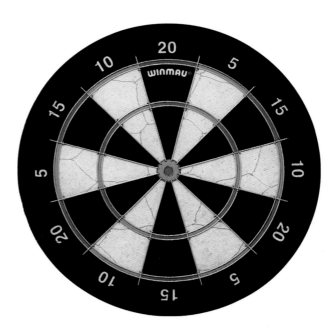

The London Fives (or 'Clock') dartboard. (Photo: WINMAU Dartboard Co. Ltd)

still enjoy darts either under supervision by their parents or by using safer forms of the game that feature magnets or Velcro.

For well over 100 years, modern darts has been a feature of pub, club and home life in England and since the 1930s in Northern Ireland, Wales and Scotland. In the past five decades, the sport has developed to such an extent that it has become a global sport.

Electronic or Soft-Tip Darts – Part of the Family

While this book concentrates on the standard, English dart game as played throughout the world and administered by the BDO, PDC and globally by the

WDF, it is recognized that other, more technical versions of the game exist.

Since the 1980s, electronic versions of the game played with soft-tipped darts have been developed, particularly in parts of the USA and in Japan. For electronic darts, the same darts are used, except that the points are made from a tough durable material (acetyl) rather than steel. In many areas of these two countries, soft-tip darts is more popular than the English steel-tip game. In parts of Europe where the traditional game of darts never reached, the electronic, pay-to-play game has been adopted. The machine, the target area of which is the same size and design as the standard, deducts the scores automatically as each dart strikes the scoring area.

The basic principles of how to play,

A soft-tip dart. (Photo: WINMAU Dartboard Co. Ltd.)

stand and throw are the same. Thus, soft-tip players will benefit from this book.

It must be said that, despite the best efforts of a number of electronic darts manufacturers, this version of the sport has yet to make any substantial inroads into the darting communities of the British Isles. The British simply do not take kindly to their game being messed about with.

The Game of 501

This book concentrates almost exclusively on what is known as the game of 501 as played on the standard (trebles) dartboard and regulated by the BDO and PDC in accordance with rules determined by those governing bodies. Although described in depth in Chapter 5, the game is basically one of reducing the score of 501 to zero in the least number of darts and, of course, quicker than your opponent. Each game is concluded on the double that reduces 501 exactly to nothing.

There are numerous other games that can be played on the standard dartboard, including adaptations of other sports including bowls, cricket and football but such games are rarely, if ever, featured in serious tournaments. Instead, they bring an element of fun to a casual evening of darts or are a pleasant digression for the serious player during his or her lengthy practice sessions. A small selection of these alternative dart games is included in Chapter 10.

There are also a few regional dartboards, such as the small Manchester Board, the Yorkshire Board and the London Fives board with thriving leagues, playing to different rules than those now considered to be standard. Examples of these dartboards and one or two others you may come across in your darts travels are referred to in Chapter 11.

Darts Today

So, a very warm welcome to the great sport of darts.

Darts can be played successfully and enjoyably regardless of age, gender, ability, disability, class or creed. It can be played anywhere, down the pub or club, at an academy, at small venues or large auditoria and in the home. It can be played on your own, one-against-one or in teams. Darts is both a social recreation and a serious sport where the financial rewards for professional players are today higher than ever before. Thus, darts can take you as short a distance as from your home to your local pub or club or to the four corners of the world.

The level at which each participant plays is his or her choice but, of course, to succeed at any level demands dedication, commitment and a full understanding of the rules, protocols and etiquette. It is easy to learn but, as professional Bobby George often tells players new to the game: 'Darts is an easy game to play but a difficult game to play well.'

Thus, the purpose of this book is not only to help you all learn how to play darts and master the basics but also to help those of you who are looking to improve your current game and maybe even look to becoming a professional – a star of the future.

CHAPTER 2

GETTING STARTED

Unsurprisingly, the majority of adults are introduced to darts in their local pub or club by engaging in a game at the invitation of friends or associates already familiar with the social benefits of 'throwing a few arrows'. Others may be introduced to the sport via a parent or older sibling who is already playing at, and possibly for, their local pub. They may even have played darts from an early age at home.

Darts is played in a spirit of friendly rivalry in the casual ambience of the pub but the more serious competitive nature of the sport will be experienced if the player progresses to a team format. There may be one or more levels of league play ('A' and 'B' teams) and beyond local pub and club leagues lies the Super League structure. Beyond that are the county-level leagues from which players are selected for their ultimate goal, which is either to play for their country or to move into the ranks of the professionals and have the opportunity to earn a good living from the sport they love – or both.

In addition, as darts is an indoor sport it can be played almost anywhere. For those looking to play at home, there is guidance below detailing how to create a professional set-up under your own roof.

Choosing a Pub, Club or Academy

Deciding on a pub or club might be a simple matter of popping down to your local or, as above, joining a parent or sibling at their local and developing a love of darts. For aspiring players aged under eighteen, there are a growing number of darts academies around the country that cater for and train young people away

from the perceived bad influence of playing in a pub.

These academies are usually run by experienced players and are supported by local companies and/or members of the darts industry, who provide sponsorship in the form of equipment and clothing. These companies are fully aware these young players are not only their future customers but may be among the next wave of new players to attain semi-professional or professional level and, in effect, secure the future of the sport.

Details of some of the academies available to young people are shown in the appendix Useful Contacts.

The Venue – What Will I Find There?

When you go to play darts in the pub, club or academy there should be nothing for you to do except arrive with your darts. The playing area, or in some cases the playing areas, consisting of the

A typical pub oche set-up in Chelmsford, Essex. (Photo: Chippix)

Youngsters learning to play at a Steve Brown Darts Academy in 2014. (Photo: Steve Brown)

or a raised oche (sometimes called the throw line or toe line). The oche length is determined by a plumb line dropped from the bullseye; that is from the face of the board to the floor, from which point the approved distance is measured horizontally along the floor at right angles to the wall.

Where that measurement terminates is marked with the oche line, behind which the player stands to throw his or her darts. No player is allowed to step over this line until they have completed their throw. However, players are allowed to move along the oche and imaginary extensions of that line in either direction as far as they wish in order to have a better view of part of the dartboard that may be obstructed by one of their preceding darts.

Playing Darts at Home

If you are keen to set up your own darts area at home and practise to your heart's content, it is very important you ensure it complies with standard rules of play. If

dartboard, the oche (or throw-line) and lighting, will all be in place, set up in accordance with the standard rules of play.

Wherever you play darts you will find the dartboard (or dartboards) hung on the wall with the centre of the bullseye exactly 5ft 8in (1.73m) from the floor. The 20 segment will be at the top of the board and, vertically below it at the bottom of the board you will see the 3 segment. Each dartboard will be firmly affixed to the wall or be securely fitted in a two-door dartboard cabinet. This ensures that there is no movement of the dartboard, either during play or when darts are taken out after each throw.

The dartboard will usually be in a position that affords other players, customers or members to see the action. In some pubs or clubs where the sport is extremely popular, you may well find a dedicated darts room.

The standard distance from which to throw a dart is 7ft 9¼in (2.37m). This is marked by either a fixed line in the floor

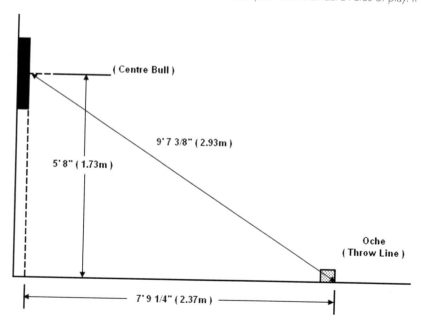

(Centre Bull)

9' 7 3/8" (2.93m)

5' 8" (1.73m)

Oche
(Throw Line)

7' 9 1/4" (2.37m)

A standard oche set-up. (Image: David King/Darts501.com)

you plan to play on a regular basis and perhaps join a club or league you will put yourself at a distinct disadvantage if, say, the length of your oche at home is an inch or two shorter than you would find at the pub. Probably the only thing you cannot replicate at home is the background noise.

If you have any neighbours then consideration should be given to them. Do not hang your dartboard on a party wall. Even if your neighbours are darts fans, they will definitely not appreciate the thud, thud, thud of dart after dart hitting the target.

As far as safety of your own family is concerned, ensure the dartboard is not hung on the back of a door. Apart from you not being able to secure the board properly on a door, someone might be seriously injured if they open it and walk in while you are in mid-throw. This warning given, you might wish to consider setting the whole thing up in the garage or shed instead.

Spacial Requirement

Wherever you decide to set up your dartboard, you must consider your actual spacial requirements. You will need sufficient space to move comfortably around, especially if you intend to invite family and/or friends round to play. A minimum area of approximately 12ft long by 5ft to 6ft wide (3.66m long by 1.52 to 1.83m wide) is recommended, which will comprise the darts-throwing area with additional space away from the oche to store your equipment.

At home, as in the pub or club, eating and/or drinking during darts play is not advisable. However, if you decide that it should be part of your practice regime (perhaps awarding yourself your favourite snack for a good checkout) then you must ensure that any food or drink is placed on a small table away from the throwing area. Remember too that if you have eaten before you practice, wash your hands thoroughly. Sticky fingers can seriously affect your throw. Also, make sure that your hands are dry before you pick up your darts.

Hanging your Dartboard

In deciding where to hang your dartboard, it must be in a position not impeded by anything. Do not place the board in a corner, at right angles to another wall that runs parallel to the throw. To do so would mean you will not be able to move along the oche in that direction if you need to adjust your position to see a target that has become obscured by a preceding dart.

Your positioning should also take into account the chance that your throwing action might be impeded by sunlight streaming in through a window, which could affect your vision and cast shadows across the board. Simply closing curtains will not work as this would reduce the amount of natural light in the room.

The majority of today's bristle dartboards come complete with a kit that includes everything you need, except a screwdriver, to fix it to the wall. The kit includes a bracket, mounting screws and three small 'legs' that are screwed to the reverse of the dartboard to prevent it coming into direct contact with the wall. To help preserve the wall, a dartboard surround is recommended which will substantially reduce, but will not prevent entirely, damage occasioned by errant darts.

Housing your Dartboard

Alternatively, it is strongly recommended you invest in a wooden cabinet to keep your board in. These are available from any number of sources and not only help protect your wall but the doors can be closed after practice. This will protect the dartboard from potentially harmful sunlight, which can dry it and cause it to harden, and will ensure your board has the longest life possible.

Both cabinet doors will usually have scoreboards on them, which negates the use of any other, unless you wish to invest in an electronic version (See Chapter 9). However, if neither are within your financial limits for the moment then you will need to make provision for a scoreboard that is positioned so it can be seen clearly from the oche or throw line. This can take the form of a simple wipe-clean whiteboard secured to the wall, on to which scores can easily be recorded using a marker pen.

To protect your floorboards and/or carpet from possible damage from rebounding or dropped darts, you should buy a darts mat. Made of thick rubber or a similarly sturdy material, these mats come marked with the standard length of throw and possibly with other less common throw lines such as 6ft and 8ft. However, if placed over a carpet, the mat will tend to move when walked on and thereby distort your line of throw, so it is best to fix it permanently to the floor if possible.

Lighting

In darts' early days in English pubs, lighting the dartboard was often by way of a strategically placed paraffin lamp or candles, and in the home no special lighting was provided. Today, there is no reason why any dartboard anywhere should not be illuminated properly.

Efficient lighting is, of course, automatically provided at darts venues but at home you must do your utmost to ensure the entire surface of the board is lit up so that all segments can be seen clearly and that there is absolutely no shadow. If there is evidence of shadow obscuring your view of any part of the target, you will never be able to play at your best.

Thus it is recommended that a strong spotlight be set up in the ceiling of your room, positioned in such a way that it points directly towards the board and lights the whole surface. Make sure that it is fixed high enough to ensure there is no risk of it being struck by darts and check the lamp is shielded properly so it does not shine in your eyes during play.

The Circumluminator, one of the modern ways of ensuring efficient lighting of the surface of the dartboard. (Photo: Scott Harrison, Nuvolux Incorporated)

Alternatively, if you have the finance, you (or your pub or club) could invest in one of the many manufactured darts lighting systems, of which the Circumluminator shown here is but one example.

Ready to Play!

So, you've set up your darts area at home, replicating as closely as possible any standard oche you might find anywhere in the country. You are now ready (subject to deciding on the right equipment for you) to play one of the best and most social indoor sports ever invented.

Clearly, when beginning to learn how to play darts, you will need an effective instructional manual to teach you the rudiments from novice up to advanced level. Of course, you already have that in this guide but for those wishing to learn more about the history of the sport and the lives of professional players, a short list of suggested further reading is provided at the end of this book.

The Rules of the Sport

There are at present two national

controlling bodies for darts in the UK, the Professional Darts Corporation (PDC), existing primarily to support professional players, and the British Darts Organisation (BDO), which functions nationally under the banner of 'Darts for All'. Both sets of rules are very similar but, given that the BDO has existed since 1973, any specific rules quoted in this book will be those of that organization. (If you wish to read the full, extensive rules of these two organizations, the website addresses can be found under the Useful Contacts section.)

Thus, this section contains a simplified description of what the game of darts involves and how it is played. The various terms and expressions commonly used in the game are outlined in the text but their meanings and derivations are explained fully in the Glossary.

The Basic Equipment – Dartboard

Until the early to mid 1970s, the majority of dartboards were manufactured from wood, usually poplar or elm, both being soft woods which are easy to cut and shape. The subtleness of the wood also ensured the incoming darts penetrated

The logo of the British Darts Organisation (BDO).

PDC

PROFESSIONAL DARTS CORPORATION

The logo of the Professional Darts Corporation (PDC).

the target sufficiently deeply to enable them to stay in.

It is easy to see from a drying slice of tree trunk how the circular pattern of the rings and the radial cracks that appear led to the present design of the dartboard; the latter indicating the segmentation of the board.

The dartboard featuring both the double and treble rings was declared 'standard' by the then newly-formed National Darts Association (NDA) in London in 1925. A modern example is shown here. However, in some areas, and especially in the north of England, the decree from London was viewed as an imposition and ignored. Thus, the trebles board was not an overnight success, initially having to compete with other differently designed existing regional dartboards, which continued to be used in some localities. For more information about regional targets see Chapter 11.

Back in the 1920s and 1930s, wooden dartboards reigned supreme but it is interesting to note that among other materials used in their manufacture at that time were compressed paper, clay, cardboard, cork and gum. It is a total myth that, as has been alluded to in some dart books, dartboards have ever been constructed from pig-bristle or horsehair.

During the 1930s, the NODOR

A slice of a tree trunk showing the familiar radial marks similar to those on a dartboard. (Photo: Author's Darts Archive)

A modern dartboard. (Photo: WINMAU Dartboard Co. Ltd)

company, then based in the east end of London, filed a patent for what was to become known as the 'bristle' dartboard, manufactured from compressed sisal fibre (the same material as that used to make ropes). This type of dartboard was originally very expensive but became increasingly popular in the 1970s, especially after elm tree supplies were decimated by Dutch elm disease and particularly once the BDO introduced a rule stating that bristle dartboards were the only ones to be used in its tournaments.

Today, whatever dartboard is used in pubs and clubs for formal or informal matches, it must conform with the approved dimensions for tournament/ competition play under BDO/PDC rules. The image of the standard dartboard shown here is the most common and recognizable target in the sport of darts. Eighteen inches (45.7cm) in diameter and with a scoring area with a diameter of 13¼in (33.7cm) the dartboard features twenty segments (numbered 1 to 20) that appear to be in a random order.

You will also notice around the circumference of the target there is a ring of small segments, only ³⁄₈ in wide. This is the double ring and any dart landing in that tiny area will score, not surprisingly, twice the value of the number. Then, midway between the double ring and the outer bullseye, there is another ring, the treble ring: this is worth three times the value of the number of the main segment.

The centre of the dartboard, like the majority of target sports, is known as the bullseye. Up until the introduction of the standard board this was the highest possible score, 50 points, the same as its ancestor archery. The bullseye also counts as double 25. In addition, the modern dartboard has an 'outer bull', which scores 25 points. Thus, when the treble ring was introduced, the highest score attainable on a dartboard increased to 60 points (3 × 20 points), moving up from the centre of the board to more than 3in above the bullseye.

The only non-scoring part of a standard dartboard is that area between the outer wire of the double ring and the edge of the board. Its purpose is three-fold: firstly

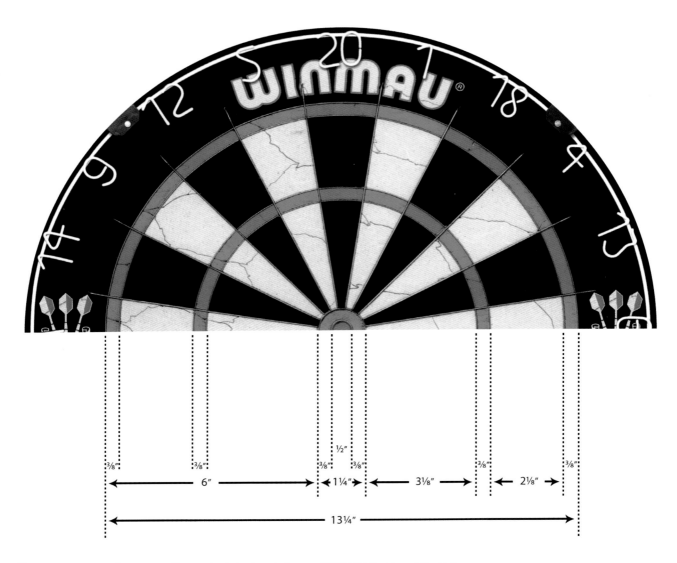

The measurements of segments of a standard dartboard. (Image: WINMAU Dartboard Co. Ltd)

to provide a safe area for darts that miss the scoring area to land rather than hit the wall (this is known as 'off the island'). Secondly, it provides sufficient space for the number ring, which indicates the main value of each segment, to be placed and clearly seen. Thirdly, it affords space for manufacturers to print their product name and company logo or, in the case of personalized dartboards, *your* name if so desired.

The numbers on a dartboard are not sequential. High numbers have much lower numbers either side. For example, the 20 segment (by far the most popular part of the target for the majority of players) is flanked by 5 to the left and 1 to the right. Similarly, at the bottom of the board, the 19 segment is wedged between 7 and 3, while the 16 segment has 8 on one side and 7 on the other. The purpose of this devious sequencing is to ensure that accuracy is rewarded and inaccuracy punished. Thus, failure to hit the intended target, say the 20 segment, will inevitably result in a much lower score, which might well require a change of tactics on the part of the player and make the game take longer to complete.

The segments are separated by a framework of wires, often called the 'spider', which ensures that each number or its double or treble values are properly delineated. Therefore, there can be no disputing which segment of the dartboard each dart has landed in. For the most modern dartboards, the wired 'spider' has been replaced by thin metal blades embedded in the board. Although the segments can still be seen clearly, the thinness of the structure allows for better accuracy, giving the player a slightly bigger target at which to aim. It also reduces the possibility of a 'bounce out': a situation in which an incoming dart hits the wire and rebounds to the floor, of course scoring no points at all.

As can be seen clearly from the image of the standard dartboard above, each scoring segment is coloured either black, white, green or red. The larger areas of the 20 segment are coloured black and those of the 1 segment next to it are white, and this continues in a clockwise direction around the board. Notice too that the double and treble segments of the 20 are coloured red and those of the 1 are green, and that this too continues in sequence round the board. The outer bull (which scores 25 points) is green and the bullseye (50 points) red. The non-scoring area around the target is coloured black. These comprise the standard colours of a modern dartboard.

As the majority of darts players score on the 20 for most of their games, that segment and the area around the treble 20 (commonly known as 'the red bit' or 'lipstick') take a lot of punishment and can begin to show signs of wear. Thus, to avoid damage and prolong the life of the dartboard, it must be turned occasionally. This is done by removing the numbered ring, moving the board two segments round and then replacing the ring. The board is moved round two segments to ensure the standard colour pattern as described above is maintained. (There have been several different colours of segment used in the past, including just black and yellow. However, such variances

are found nowadays only on children's boards.)

In the majority of top darts tournaments today, the dartboard is often replaced after every match. It may also be replaced if both players (or the teams) request it and, naturally, if the board is damaged during play.

It is essential all players familiarize themselves with the layout of the board and learn the position and value of each and every number, every double, every treble, the 25 and bullseye. Without that basic knowledge you will never become a proficient player at any level.

The Basic Equipment – Darts

Theories abound about how the dart evolved. Some believe the first darts were made from broken arrows, which were sharpened and then thrown at the ends of wine casks. Others argue crossbow bolts were the precursor of the modern dart, or that 'puff and dart' started it all in the sixteenth century. Surprisingly though, the truth is that the original wooden darts

used in the game we recognize today as the sport of darts were not English or even British, but French!

The first darts used by the masses in England were imported from France in the mid to late Victorian period initially to satisfy demand from fairgrounds and subsequently by toy manufacturers. It is not surprising then that they were called 'French darts'.

Made entirely of wood, with a pin or metal point in one end and three or four turkey feathers glued to the other end to provide the flight, these proved extremely popular and were often supplied by pub licensees free of charge to customers in order to encourage more men (primarily) to play darts and thus, hopefully, drink more beer.

As the game became increasingly popular in the 1920s and 1930s, light engineering companies in England turned their attention to darts and manufactured the first brass-barrelled example, eventually selling them in packs of three. (French darts had been available singularly.) Brass darts barrels were produced in hundreds of shapes, sizes and weights and quickly took over from the

Early wooden French darts. (Photo: Author's Darts Archive)

Brass darts ruled the dartboards for many decades until the advent of tungsten in the early 1970s. (Photo: Author's Darts Archive)

French dart as the most popular form used in general play. Despite this, French darts are still available from specialist dealers but are never used in serious tournament play.

Brass darts were originally fitted with cane shafts, slit crossways at the back end, into which a folded card or paper flight could be inserted. For those who still preferred feather flights, brass barrels were also manufactured with threads that would take an adaptor, into which such flights could be inserted. Brass was to remain the dart of choice until the early 1970s, when tungsten alloy darts (usually just called 'tungstens') were introduced and the 'tungsten revolution' began.

The benefit of tungsten is that it is denser than brass and so what had previously been a bulky brass dart of, say, 28g became a super-slim tungsten model of equal weight. Tungsten on its own is brittle, and thus more or less impossible to machine, so manufacturers create an alloy by combining tungsten powder with, usually, nickel or copper. They then convert the resultant material into manageable tungsten billets that are easily converted into dart barrels.

Because they are thinner, tungsten darts do not take up as much room when in the dartboard as the larger brass examples and therefore leave more space for incoming darts. Thus, if you were playing with brass darts and you hit a treble 20 with your first dart, it would not have left much room in the treble 20 segment for the two subsequent darts. Indeed, the thickness of the barrel of the brass dart might well obscure the rest of that segment. By leaving more space for following darts, tungstens make a 'maximum' (three treble 20s – a score of 180 points) more achievable but, of course, this will only be achieved by practice.

Today, tungstens are the choice of champions, established darters and new players alike. Brass darts, rarely used in any level of competition these days, have been consigned to a supplementary role, being supplied in family sets or as the introductory darts used by young and older novice players before, after learning to play and love the game, moving on to tungstens.

OK. You are now ready to choose your equipment.

CHAPTER 3

CHOOSING YOUR EQUIPMENT

While the choice of dartboards is relatively straightforward: a top-quality bristle dartboard for serious play and practice, coiled paper or magnetic dartboards for family fun or boards and darts of Velcro for the very young, when it comes to selecting your first, and subsequent sets of darts and related accessories, you do need some guidance.

In this chapter, I provide advice on choosing those most essential items, your darts, plus their component parts, the flights and stems.

Darts

The range of darts available to you is, to say the least, very confusing, if not bewildering. The only issue you do not have to decide is the material from which the barrels are made. To mix it with the best, the main constituent must be tungsten. That is, unless you wish to remain a novice and use much cheaper and less effective brass darts.

The range of tungsten darts available is seemingly endless with, for example, at the time of writing, weights (of the barrel) ranging from 13.5g (lightest) to 40g (heaviest). In organized tournaments, under BDO rules, the darts used cannot weigh more than 50g and the overall length of the darts from tip of point to tip of flight should not exceed 12in (30.5cm).

Prices vary in accordance with the type of product and construction. The general advice for novice players is to begin with a medium-weighted dart of, say, 20 to 23g, with a medium length stem (2in/5.1cm) and standard-shaped flights.

A small selection of the styles and weights of darts available are shown here.

Most darts have a rigid, fixed point, although spring-loaded darts are preferred by some players. Spring-loaded darts are constructed in such a way that the point is free, which means that when the dart hits the board the point penetrates the target, while the rest of the dart continues to move forward at around 35mph and hammers the point further in. This effectively reduces bounce outs.

What Dart is Best for You?

In the majority of cases, individuals decide by a process of trial and error, often over a period of time. Perhaps having no darts of their own, new darts players might borrow a set from friends at the club or pub or, in the latter, use the 'house darts'; that is a set made available for free by the licensee. But beware, 'house darts' are notoriously poor quality and are rarely if ever tungstens as such valuable darts often tend to 'walk'.

A selection of the best tungsten darts available today. (Photo: WINMAU Dartboard Co. Ltd)

By casual experimentation, the player will eventually make a judgment as to roughly the type and weight of dart he or she thinks will be best for them. Many will then rush to purchase a set on the internet but this may not be the best way forward. To ensure the very best results, a player new to the game should 'try before they buy' by seeking out and visiting a specialist shop. In such a shop customers will be able to test various types of darts and flights, and they will be able to get guidance and then decide which are the best for their style of throw.

However, it is unlikely the first set of darts you buy will stay with you throughout your darting life. As you become more confident and competent you will wish to fine tune your play which, in turn might mean a change of the style of flights, the length of the shaft or indeed demand replacement darts.

An incredible mass of information (and disinformation) about darts equipment exists on the internet, which can prove confusing, especially to the novice player. Bear in mind that the worldwide web does not have any advantage over you physically stepping into a darts suppliers' shop, discussing your requirements and then testing out any number of sets of tungstens of differing weights, with different lengths of shaft and various shapes of flights.

After toeing the oche as instructed by the shop owner, or where you feel the most comfortable when throwing your first darts under shop oche conditions, throw each one at your selected target and watch where and how it hits the board. If the darts stick in yet fall below the intended target, this indicates the darts are too heavy for your style of throw. On the other hand, if the darts land above the intended target, then the darts may be too light. You can try to rectify this by choosing a lighter, heavier or medium dart, aiming and throwing at the dartboard again and noting any improvement.

Once comfortable with your chosen darts, buy them and go to the pub or club and play. Set up a dartboard at home and play. There is nothing more important in darts than practice, practice and more practice.

Keeping the same barrels but changing the length of the shaft or the shape of your flights (or both) and experimenting will undoubtedly improve the way you and your darts perform on the oche.

As you become more experienced and accomplished you will undoubtedly need to make such changes to your darts as are necessary to adapt to your personal, developing style. As time goes by, you may indeed decide to make the most major of adjustments: changing your darts entirely.

Importantly, you must realize from day one that an expensive set of darts will not guarantee success or turn you into a great player overnight. It is said that a workman is only as good as his tools. In sport, a sportsman or sportswoman is only as good as his or her equipment, their natural talent and commitment.

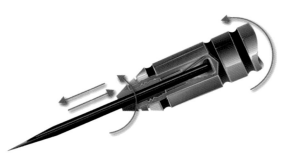

A moving point spring-loaded dart. (Photo: WINMAU Dartboard Co. Ltd)

Trying before he buys. A player tests the darts available at Darts Corner. (Photo: Darts Corner)

The component parts of a modern dart. (Photo: WINMAU Dartboard Co. Ltd/ Suzan Ahmet)

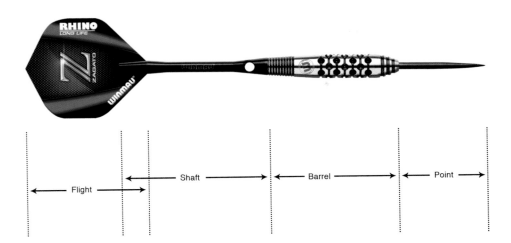

Flight   Shaft   Barrel   Point

Component Parts – Flights

The purpose of a flight is to stabilize the dart once thrown to ensure it has the best chance of hitting its intended target; the desired segment of the dartboard. It is therefore important that whatever flights you use they are kept in pristine condition or replaced.

In the early twentieth century, flights were made from paper or card – or handmade from, for example, cigarette cards – and slipped into cane shafts. They may also have comprised turkey feathers, which were integral to the wooden or 'French' dart. Nowadays, feather or paper flights are a rarity, nearly all players today opting to use 'plastic' flights made from polypropylene that come conveniently packed in sets of three. Some of the most popular shapes of flight are shown here. That shown as the 'standard' flight has been the most popular since the mid-1970s.

In addition to different shapes, changes in the manufacturing process can give the flights a dimpled appearance. The numbers of different designs available are countless and include saucy images, holograms, surreal sci-fi creatures, the name and badge of your favourite football team, lager, beer and spirit advertising, flags of all nations, animals, cars and company logos. The list is endless. A small selection of designs are shown in this chapter. You can even have your own name and design featured on your own flights. Information about where to go for such a service is given in the Useful Contacts section.

Some darts manufacturers provide 'flight selector' packs: sets of various shapes of flight. This enables the player to experiment to ascertain whether or not something other than 'standard' will aid his or her game. However, in general, it seems to be the case that once a player has decided on the type of flight to use, they tend to stick with it.

When a player experiences a 'bounce out', where a second or third dart appears to bounce off the surface of the board, this is often not the case. It is usually that an incoming dart has struck a dart already in the target and bounces off that. Such events can be reduced significantly by the use of a 'flight saver' or 'protector', a small, carefully crafted metal cap that fits over the top end of each flight and deflects following darts. Hopefully, the direction is into the board rather than on to the floor. These protectors also have a secondary use, which is to help prolong the life of each flight. However, this product cannot protect flights from damage caused by the actions of darts players who insist on pulling all three of their darts out of the board by the flights in a single-handed, grabbing movement.

When players reach high levels of skill and join a Super League to further improve their skills or play for their county or in major tournaments, they will often be seen examining their flights after every

A selection of shapes and designs of modern flights. Top: Standard flights. Bottom (left to right); Arrowhead, Tomahawk, Fantail, Pear, Slim. (Photo: WINMAU Dartboard Co. Ltd)

throw and replacing them if there are signs of any problems or damage. It is not unusual for serious darts players to discard their flights after every match.

Component Parts – Shafts

The shaft (also sometimes referred to as the 'stem'), while lengthening the dart, also has the vital function of linking the barrel to the flight; the shaft screwing firmly into the barrel and the grooves at the other end enabling the flight to be pushed into the shaft and secured.

Shafts are manufactured from several kinds of material including nylon, polycarbonate and aluminium. Nylon shafts are made from a multi-material polymer that allows each one to be both flexible and extra tough to withstand the rigours of the modern game. Nylon shafts can also be purchased with a spring at the flight end. This small spring, pushed up once the flight is inserted into the shaft, locks the flight in place and can even prevent 'Robin Hooding', where a following dart becomes stuck in the shaft of an earlier dart.

To increase flight grip, some nylon shafts are available with aluminium tops. This also increases the ability of incoming darts to be led into the dartboard, thereby potentially reducing the number of bounce outs. Some shafts feature an aluminium rotary (or revolving) top. Again this affords extra flight grip but also free rotation of the flight, which allows incoming darts to easily pass the flight and thereby helps to improve the players' overall score.

A small selection of the wide variety of shafts available. (Photo: WINMAU Dartboard Co. Ltd.)

Shafts are also available made entirely of aluminium and anodized aluminium. They can even be diamond-cut and/or laser-etched. Aluminium alloys are often used in the production of shafts as they offer a much-improved strength-to-weight ratio over plastic-based alternatives. Shafts are made on computer-controlled machines, which typically produce several sets each minute. Slots measuring less than twelve thousandths of an inch are cut to secure the flights and a cross hole is drilled to enable a dart point to be used to tighten the shaft into its barrel.

If you read in a catalogue that a shaft is 'anodized aluminium', this means that an electrical coating process known as 'anodizing' has been subsequently applied to the aluminium shaft. The dart shaft is made the 'anode' in an electrolytic cell and once the electrical current is applied, a coating of aluminium oxide forms on the surface of the shaft, which is both hard wearing and can absorb dyes to colour the surface. The lengths of shaft available usually range from 15mm (the shortest) to in excess of 65mm. They are also produced in a variety of colours.

In the flight section above, a 'flight Selector' pack was mentioned that enables you to experiment with different styles and shapes of flight. Some darts manufacturers also produce a pack that combines different flights with differing lengths of stem. One company describes this as a 'tune-up kit', a product that enables you to help refine your throw and decide what is right for you.

Other Darts Accessories

There is a myriad of other accessories available to players, including darts sharpeners, wallets and cases, clothing, wristbands, sighting aids, ear plugs and point sharpeners – even a hi-tech laser beam to help you mark the oche line. There is also an ever-expanding market for personalized flights, shafts and boards. The list is endless. However, that is for later (See Chapter 9).

For now, armed only with your finely-tuned darts, it is time to learn the rudiments of the sport.

A flight selector pack. (Photo: WINMAU Dartboard Co. Ltd)

PART 2

SKILLS AND TECHNIQUES

CHAPTER 4

HOW TO PLAY – THE BASICS

Now you have chosen your darts, have found a venue and/or installed a dartboard in your home, it is time to familiarize yourself with the basic skills to enable you to play and enjoy the game.

This chapter teaches you how to grip a dart, how to stand at the oche (the 'stance') and how to throw and properly release each dart correctly to give you the very best chance of hitting your intended target. It also

suggests the best clothing to wear on the oche.

Those people who will tell you it does not matter how you hold a dart, how you stand or how you throw have a lot to learn and could

Darts' smart image from 1925 – the Regent Tavern darts team of Bow, London. (Photo: Scottish & Newcastle)

benefit, as you are doing, by reading this book.

To become proficient at any sport you must have a grasp of the fundamentals before you can look to improvement and, of course, the ultimate pleasure of playing consistently good darts and winning matches.

These basics will help you understand both the game and how to play it. As in all sports, standard rules apply but as your skills develop you will undoubtedly fine tune your game in any number of ways. How to improve on the basics is the subject of Chapter 6.

Before we move on to the grip, stance and throw there is one matter that must be dealt with first.

Luck

I'd like to state at the outset that luck plays no part in darts, or indeed any other sport. Very occasionally unexpected situations may arise, such as your opponent missing a chance to win the match, giving you the opportunity to hit the winning double. You might consider this to be a lucky event but it is not. It is an opening afforded to you by the inefficiency, temporary or otherwise, of your opponent.

How to Dress for Darts

This may sound strange bearing in mind that it is 'only darts' but before we move on to learning how to throw darts properly, we must pause a while to think about how we dress for a match.

Many years ago, men used to play in suits and ties, as evidenced by old photographs and newsreels, but those days are now long gone. Today, the emphasis for every player, male or female, is on comfort.

Comfort is not only fundamental but, I believe, crucial, especially in relation to the freedom of movement of the throwing arm.

When playing at your local pub or club, there is unlikely to be a dress code as there is in more formal matches so dress in a casual, relaxed way that usually reflects the laid-back nature of such venues. Serious darts clubs and

organizations often impose a 'no jeans' rule and ban headgear (except for religious reasons).

But why shouldn't a darts player adopt a very smart appearance? It can go a long way to improving self-confidence. That may be true but you can still look smart wearing casual-smart clothes. Casual, open-neck, short-sleeved shirts or tops are favoured by most male and female darts players because they are less restrictive than long-sleeved shirts or tops and allow freedom of movement for your throwing arm and wrist, something that is so important at every level.

Martin Adams, Three times BDO World Champion and three times winner of the WINMAU World Masters. (Photo: Tip Top Pics Ltd)

Trina Gulliver MBE, nine times Women's World Darts Champion. (Photo: Tip Top Pics Ltd)

While jeans tend to be the norm at a casual level, trousers tend to be *de rigeur* under more formal rules and are adopted by both sexes. As with shirts and tops, trousers or slacks must be practical and comfortable and not be too tight or restrict movement in any way, particularly when on the oche. Of course, women could opt to wear a dress but this is rarely seen in darts at the top level. At a casual level, dresses are sometimes worn but jeans or slacks predominate.

Pockets should be kept clear of any bulky items such as a wallet or a bunch of keys as any level of discomfort will tend to affect not only your stance but also your throw. Entrust those items to a good friend while you play.

Although trainers are not approved of at the higher levels of competition, most casual players choose footwear that is comfortable and will ensure stability and balance when standing at the oche. Socks should also be comfortable and not restrict the feet or ankles.

Everyone wears jewellery to a greater or lesser extent, some professionals to such an extreme that they appear covered in 'bling'. But look closely. You will see that very little jewellery is worn on the throwing hand or arm. Any such body ornaments can affect your throw.

If you are superstitious and usually wear, say, a bracelet on the wrist of your throwing arm, then merely transfer it to your other wrist for the duration of the match.

The King of Bling, Bobby George. In a match, Bobby would never wear 'bling' on his throwing arm. (Photo: Patrick Chaplin/Bobby George/Wendy Balic)

Keep the throwing arm, hand and wrist clear of any potential obstructions, except perhaps a wedding or friendship ring.

As for neckwear, it is recommended that you wear only light necklaces or chains as these too can become restrictive and uncomfortable as a match goes on. Nearly every player who typically wears a watch on the wrist of their throwing arm removes it while playing darts. Any unexpected movement of the watch, bracelet or bangle or any other kind of wrist wear will have a detrimental effect on your

Rod Harrington, the Prince of Style. (Photo: Author's Darts Archive/David King)

Fortunately, he matches his exuberance with a top level of skill, playing fantastic darts.

The Grip

This is simply how you hold a dart.

Usually the recommended starting point for players new to the game is to lay the darts on a table and then pick one up with your natural playing hand. It is very likely that you will use the same grip as you would do if picking up a pen or pencil. This being the case, you will note that you are holding your dart between the thumb, the index finger and the second finger, as shown in the diagram.

In most cases the thumb automatically finds the centre of gravity but if you are uncertain where this is then you can determine it by carefully placing a dart across the top of an extended index finger and moving the dart to one side or the other until it balances without a hint of it falling off. With your playing hand, grip the dart as described above with your thumb exactly at the position of the centre of gravity.

Finding the centre of gravity will mean the weight of each dart will be evenly distributed as you prepare to throw. It also ensures that you will be properly 'flighting' each dart you throw and thus, provided you adhere to the other basic advice relating to stance and throw, you will have more control over where each dart lands.

In what is regarded as the 'standard grip', the index finger is placed on top of the barrel with the second finger extended practically to the end of the barrel. Equal pressure should be applied to the barrel of the dart by both fingers and the thumb. This establishes a firm but relatively light grip: not too light as this may cause the dart to fall out of your hand and not too tight as this may ultimately affect your ability to release the dart properly.

Practise your grip by holding the dart in

throw whether you actually realise it or not.

What you wear for a match normally comes down to personal choice. Although some players you will face will appear to be making some kind of fashion statement, they are there to beat you – to win the game.

There are those professional players who want to be noticed; to be identified apart from the pack. Some years ago, England's Rod Harrington took to wearing a suit and tie on stage, removing his jacket before he threw his first dart. He was subsequently dubbed The Prince of Style. More recently, and to the other extreme, professional Peter 'Snakebite' Wright has made colour and excessive hairstyles his trademark.

Scotland's Peter Wright, the most colourful player on the PDC circuit. (Photo: Tip Top Pics Ltd)

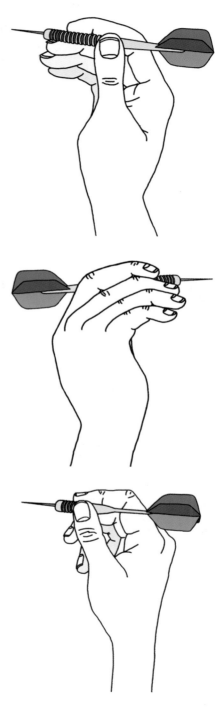

Some ways darts are held. (Illustration: Chris Barrell/Suzan Ahmet)

Ex-England International Doug McCarthy demonstrates how to hold a dart while practising at home. (Photo: Doug McCarthy)

the weight will be *behind* the grip and so you will be *throwing* the dart. If gripped at the back of the barrel, most of the weight will be *in front* of the grip which means that you will be *pushing* the dart. Using the centre of gravity as your best guide, the standard grip will ensure that the dart is 'flighted' properly towards your intended target.

Even so, when watching darts you will have noticed that no two players grip their darts in exactly the same way. There are many factors that influence the grip and these include the shape and length of the barrel, the length of the shaft and the flight design. Even the size of a player's hands might demand a slight adjustment of the standard grip.

By far the most recognizable grip of any darts player of recent times is that of five-time World Champion Eric 'The Crafty Cockney' Bristow. Eric's third finger actually touches the point of the dart and his little finger is cocked and pointing upwards, as you can see from the photograph in this chapter. This is most unusual but has proved very effective. Although no longer entering competitive tournaments, Bristow continues to play in exhibitions where he remains a match for most players who care (or dare) to take him on. His reputation still precedes him.

Whatever grip you use, after experimentation or not, and whatever it may look like, the basic premise is that it must be one that always guarantees the smoothest and most accurate release of every one of your darts.

If you experience problems gripping your darts it may be that the barrels are too smooth. The answer may be to change to a set with knurled barrels. Knurls will afford you a more effective grip and, as usual, the choice available is vast. I believe looking at knurling as a solution should be pursued before turning to a cheaper alternative, such as finger wax or rubbing chalk on your darts (See Chapter 9). Applying such materials may well hinder your play rather than improve it.

your hand and then studying the position of your fingers. Put the dart down. Then pick it up again. Is your grip the same? It should be. If not, make the necessary fine adjustments. It is very important that you are, or soon become, comfortable with your grip.

Although the grip above is regarded as most commonplace, it is far from being the only one. If, as your skills improve, you decide to experiment with variations of grip then you should note the following important points relating to weight distribution.

If you alter your grip by moving it towards the front of the dart, most of

The unique Eric Bristow grip with pointing little finger. (Photo: Harrows Darts)

Any problem with grip may actually be due to the condition of your own hands. Ensure they are not greasy before a game. Have you washed your hands after that pre-match snack? No? Well, you should. Unless you utilize your fingernails in your preferred grip, clip or file down any long or rough ones as they could well catch on the barrel and directly affect your throwing action and, thereby, where the dart lands. While I realize many female darters will have long fingernails and not wish to trim them, they will have to determine what grip is best for them.

Cold hands and/or stiff fingers will place you at an instant disadvantage as these *will* affect your grip and therefore your ability to throw an accurate dart. Warm your hands by rubbing them together. Stiff fingers may be simply that and they can recover by rubbing too. More serious stiffness such as that caused by arthritis, which affects a great number of darts players as they become

Knurls aid effective grip. (Photo: WINMAU Dartboard Co. Ltd)

older, is more difficult to deal with and may require medical attention.

How to Stand at the Oche – The Stance

The darts are now in your hands and you seem to be ready. But you are not quite.

You could just stand at the oche and throw your three darts but this is 'throw and hope'. Before throwing a single dart, it is vital that you learn how to stand at the oche line. Why? Because this will ensure the most effective and accurate release of each dart as it leaves your hand on its journey to the dartboard and the specific spot on the target at which you are aiming.

When you approach the oche for the first time, stand behind the line, face the dartboard and take in what is around you. Acclimatize yourself to your position and then step forward and 'toe the line'.

Relax.

If you are right-handed, hold all three of your darts in your left (non-throwing) hand. (Reverse this process if left-handed.) Then pass one dart smoothly from your left hand to your right, bring it up to eye level and throw it towards the bullseye. (Do not worry about actually hitting any specific segment at this stage.) Repeat with the second and third darts. Become accustomed to the rhythm of passing each dart to your throwing hand and then throwing each in turn at the target.

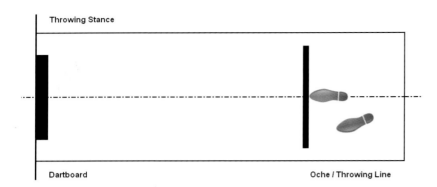

Position of feet at the oche showing lining up with the centre of the dartboard. (Image: David King/Darts501.com)

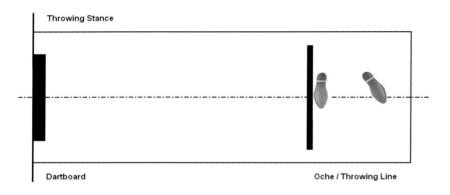

A different way of positioning your feet at the oche. (Image: David King/Darts501.com)

How did you do? Were the darts grouped nicely?

More importantly, when you were throwing your darts did you notice which parts of your body moved? If not, repeat the process and make a note. What moved? Your throwing arm? Good. A leg? Your head? Your non-throwing arm? All bad. When throwing darts absolutely nothing should move except your throwing arm, your wrist and the fingers releasing each dart.

When you watch participants in other target sports such as archery or shooting you see no movement during the aim except the pulling back of the bow string and the release of the arrow or the pulling of the trigger. Everything else is stock still. And so it is with darts.

Any movement other than that prescribed above will affect the accuracy of your throw and, thus, the consistency of your scoring to a lesser or greater extent. Watch some players as they kick out with their non-leading leg or jump a little as the last dart is released. Watch them stick their tongue out or blink or lean to one side. The sins are multitudinous.

In my view, the more movement of the body during your throw the less chance you have of winning any decent tournaments or, if that is your plan, to become a champion. But, of course, not everyone wants to become a champion but to merely go out for an evening, play and have fun. That's fine.

How you stand at the oche is known as 'the stance' and although the variations are many, over the years one stance has been more commonly found, which as a result has become regarded by many as standard.

In order to adopt this standard stance, stand at the oche facing the dartboard. Then imagine a line drawn from a point where a plumb line from the bullseye reaches the floor and then runs along the floor in a straight line towards you until it reaches the oche line. Note the point it meets that line and place your right foot against it with your right big toe leading and pointing directly along that imaginary line towards the dartboard (see diagram). Look down and ensure that your left foot is slightly behind the right and turned outwards at an angle. (If you are left-handed/footed, then naturally you should reverse this procedure.)

In this position, move your chest around slightly so that when you raise your right arm to aim and then throw each dart, not only is your right elbow pointing at the dartboard but it is also directly positioned over your right toe. Notice too that slightly more weight will fall on your right leg and foot.

A second example of how to stand at the oche, adopted by many players, is where the right foot is placed parallel with the oche line with the left foot behind it at an angle of 45 degrees. A principle benefit of adopting this stance is that it brings the player about 6in nearer to the target.

Many darts players merely adapt a stance that feels right for them from the start – one that works fine and produces results – and so they stay with it. Others experiment and over time customize their original stance more than once until they are happy.

If during practice you group your three darts well, score a significantly high number of points or hit the desired double with your first or second dart, pause once you have thrown your last

SightRight. (Photo: WINMAU Dartboard Co. Ltd)

dart and before you retrieve them from the dartboard. Look down. Make a mental note of where you are standing and then, when you throw your next three darts, stand in exactly the same position.

If you are happy with your stance, feel comfortable, there is no imbalance and every part of your body, except your throwing arm, stays stock still then your darts will fly accurately and true.

It will come as no surprise to any player to learn that for every perceived or actual problem there is a solution. So, if you are experiencing problems aligning yourself with the board there is a product, called SightRight, that can help. Once the product is set up in accordance with the instructions, you test your usual stance and throwing position. If it does not align to the marks on the SightRight, correct your position so that the centre line appears dead straight. Then correct your sighting fault and stand in the perfectly aligned position time after time.

This product not only ensures that you stand in the same position every time but also helps improve accuracy and straightens the entry of your darts into the dartboard. It can also reduce blocked targets dramatically as your darts will be entering the board straight and not landing across the target.

How to Throw your Darts

Having chosen the darts that are right for you, learned the grip and the stance and dressed appropriately for the oche, all that is left is to ensure that you master how to throw your darts.

At first sight this might seem easy: just step up to the oche and throw three darts. Easy.

No it isn't.

Throwing darts demands as much effort and concentration as any other part of your game, perhaps more. Perfecting a smooth, fluid action of the right (or left) arm that propels each dart exactly to its intended target is vital.

As always, prepare yourself mentally as you approach the oche. Learn to file away at the back of your mind in a section marked 'for later' any personal issues you may have that have nothing to do with darts. If the pub or club is noisy, you must lock out the cacophony of sound. This is not the easiest thing to do but it is essential as any and all distractions will otherwise directly affect your performance.

Step up to the line relaxed and confident.

Once at the oche, check your stance and grip. Hold all three darts in your left (or right) hand and pass the first of them into your playing hand. Then slowly bring the arm up so the dart is into the sighting position level with your right (or left) eye, almost, but not actually, touching your cheek. The closer you are to your cheek without touching it the better as this will increase the accuracy of the alignment of the eye and your dart with the intended target – the line of sight.

Some players pull their darts back too far, others not far enough. Not far enough means you will never properly align with the target, while too far means you may actually lose sight of your dart. The dart *must* be visible out of the corner of your eye so you can see it while also focusing on the intended target – the dartboard and the segment you are aiming for.

The throw is primarily about hand-eye coordination. However, it is also about position and control of your right (or left) arm.

When discussing the grip (above), the importance of the position of the elbow was noted. As you bring your dart up to the line of sight, ensure your elbow is pointing at the dartboard. The elbow is a pivot and bringing your arm back towards your face ensures the upper arm remains in a horizontal position throughout the entire motion of the throw. The wrist is a second pivot that allows the hand to bring the dart further back towards the right (or left) eye, ensuring that you never lose sight of it.

The target and the dart both being in view, you now take careful aim. With your elbow still pointing towards the dartboard and with no movement of any other part of your body, move your forearm forward and then, at the top of the arc described by that action (that is immediately before your arm begins its downward path) *release* the dart with a light, smooth, fluent action towards your target along the line of sight.

If you release a dart before it reaches the top of the arc it will not hit your intended target. It might be close but such an action will more or less guarantee your dart will land *above* the segment you are aiming for. Similarly, if you release your dart *after* the top of the arc and as your arm begins its downward path then the dart will inevitably hit the dartboard *below* your target, or even land off the scoring area altogether.

It may surprise you to learn that, in many cases, someone new to the sport of darts (and even where a player has been playing for years) can make the simple error of not actually looking at the intended target during the throw. Rest assured, a dart will not find its way to the right part of the dartboard without your personal guidance.

Another essential part of the throw, as you move your forearm forward, is to ensure your right elbow is tucked in. As each dart is released, the elbow has a tendency to want to jerk to the right. If this is not addressed and controlled such a jerking action is bound to disturb the fluidity of your throw and thus the direction and accuracy of each dart.

In golf, the importance of the follow-through once the ball has been struck is emphasized. So it is with darts. Players must always follow through after each

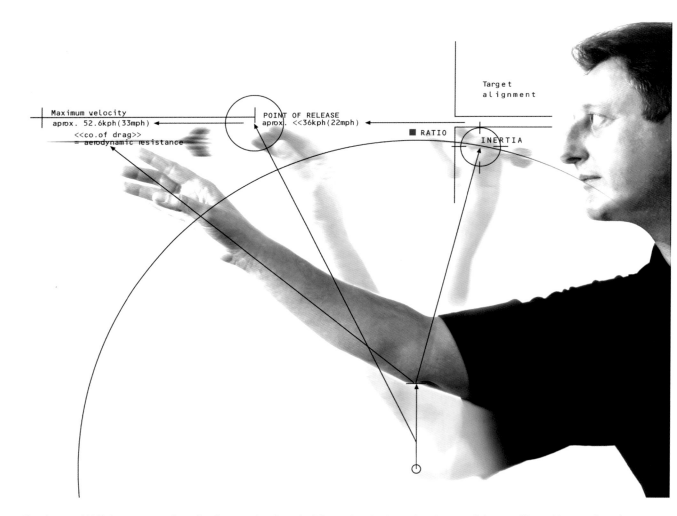

Maximum velocity
aprox. 52.6kph (33mph)

<<co.of drag>>
= aerodynamic resistance

POINT OF RELEASE
aprox. <<36kph (22mph)

■ RATIO

Target
alignment

INERTIA

Eric Bristow MBE demonstrates how the dart is sighted, pushed forward and released at the top of the arc. (Photo: Harrows Darts)

dart has been released. Failure to follow through properly will almost certainly result in a jerking or snatching action, which means that you will have effectively lost control of the direction in which your dart is travelling.

The way to prevent this happening is simply to go back to basics by standing absolutely still at the oche and restricting movement solely to the forearm, hand and wrist. Of course, you should also study the images above.

While the method of throwing darts accurately tends to follow the pattern outlined above, there are a number of players who naturally throw their darts with their right hand but line each dart up with their left eye, throwing in an arc from the left-hand side – and vice versa. These are known as 'mixed laterals'. Although their action looks awkward, it can be very effective, as proved by the successful and very long (and ongoing) career of twice Embassy World Championship runner-up Bobby George.

The average velocity of a medium weight (23–25g) dart when thrown has been estimated by some in the darts industry at approximately 35mph. However, the normal speed at which a dart is actually released tends to vary from player to player.

There are those who throw incredibly quickly and those who throw mind-numbingly slowly. In general, players new to the sport give little or no consideration to how fast or hard they throw, unless of course they miss the dartboard on a number of occasions and then have to be told to throw harder and a little faster. Most find a natural speed and rhythm that suits their personal style of play. If you throw a heavy dart, then you may have to throw harder but not necessarily faster to hit your target. Whatever speed you throw, you must ensure each dart is released at that same speed and with the same smooth action.

You will find few players will complain about an opponent who throws his or her darts fast. However, there are many who find a slow player frustrating and/or irritating to play against. If you are a naturally slow player, you must refuse to

A mixed lateral Bobby George holds and throws his darts with his right hand but lines up each throw with his left eye. (Photo: Tip Top Pics Ltd)

be rushed. Play your game. There are occasions when a fast or normal speed player deliberately tries to slow the game down in order to distract and frustrate their opponent. This and other forms of gamesmanship are discussed in Chapter 6.

Before we move on to other matters, mention must be made of a common

problem suffered by darts players and that is the 'errant third dart'. This is when, having thrown your first two darts exactly where you want them to go, the third falls short. Clearly, this could cost you the game or even the match.

Professional advice to solve this difficulty is to throw the third dart a little harder than the second dart, or to throw four darts when practising. This seems to work in most cases but if you suffer from that problem and this idea does not solve it then you will probably need to take a closer look at your grip, throw and stance to identify a more deep rooted problem. How to throw consistently accurately is probably the most difficult aspect of darts to master.

This may sound like repetition – it is – but there is no substitute for practice, practice and more practice… Practice can be boring but ways of making practice interesting (and maybe even fun) are also featured in Chapter 7.

Moving Along the Oche

If I were writing this book three or four decades ago, one of the pieces of advice I would have given would have been to never move along the oche (or 'hockey' as it was called and spelled back then). You would have been told to step up to the line, adopt your stance and throw all three darts from that position (no matter what happened); the accepted wisdom of the time being that throwing all three darts from a set, rigid position would ensure conformity of throw and thereby accuracy. Few players ever thought about moving along the oche.

However, as the sport developed during the late 1960s and 1970s it became clear that standing on the same spot could work to your disadvantage if, for example, you obscured the target

with your first or second dart. How could you possibly throw your subsequent darts effectively if you could not see the segment properly?

Some players solved the dilemma by lobbing the following dart or darts expertly over the top of the earlier ones but it soon became recognized that the best way to have a better view of the target was to move along the line. Common practice today is for players to move freely along the oche line in either direction. They may also move along beyond the oche itself provided that this is in the direction of an imaginary extension to that line.

When such a change in position is made, you must ensure that you feel comfortable with it and make allowance for the fact that by moving along the line your target will now be slightly further away. This will mean that you will have to throw darts from that distance just a little harder.

If movement along the oche does not help and your target remains obscured then, if you are aiming for high scores, for example the first dart has blocked your view of the treble 20 (60 points), you have the option of going for a 'cover shot'. In this case you stay exactly where you are and turn your attention to the next highest scoring treble: treble 19 (57 points).

However, if your obscured target is a possible winning double, you may have no option but to throw for that double and, if missed, hope that your opponent is

unable to finish so you then have a clear view on your next throw. The only instance where you have nowhere to go is if you are languishing on double 1 (commonly known as 'The Madhouse').

The necessity of having to move along the oche line does not occur during every game but you must be prepared for the possibility of one badly-placed dart threatening your ability to score highly or win the game.

Finally in this chapter, remember always that darts is akin to archery, rifle-shooting and pistol-shooting in that, unlike numerous other sports, you are alone on the oche or mark and need to concentrate solely on the business in hand – to win the game or match.

Apart from gamesmanship, there is absolutely nothing your opponent (or in team games your opponents) can do to affect your play. You can be fouled in football, snookered in snooker and tackled in rugby but in darts it is ultimately you against the dartboard.

The foregoing advice will enable you to stand more confidently at the oche and play the best game you possibly can.

OK. Let's play darts!

CHAPTER 5

THE GAME OF 501

The Basic Principles

The most common darts game played both casually and in more serious matches is 501. This is sometimes reduced to 301 for individual league and match play. In team play (up to eight players per side) the starting point is extended to 701, 801 and even 1,001.

The purpose of 501 (or any of the '-01' games) is for one player or team of players to reduce their score exactly to zero before their opponent does. However, the player or team must finish on a double that achieves zero.

Origins of '-01'

The earliest games of darts, in a form we might recognize today, consisted of players throwing one, two or three darts at a target; the one achieving the highest score winning the game. Thus each game was over very quickly. As the popularity of darts increased and players' skill levels improved, it became a little more sophisticated and the target became more complicated.

In English public houses, the original '-01' game of 301 was scored on a cribbage board. Cribbage is an old English card game invented in the seventeenth century by Sir John Suckling and was played by seemingly everyone, prince or pauper. It therefore found its way easily into the pub, where card games were usually frowned upon. Scores were derived from the value of the cards and were recorded carefully by pegging holes on the two sides of a wooden cribbage board.

Each side of the board has two rows of thirty holes, with one extra hole at each end. Scores are recorded on both sides by each player using two pegs each. To win the game, players have to successfully complete an agreed number of circuits of the cribbage board (60 holes) and finish on the extra hole that represents 'home', making a total for 'once round' of 61 points. Thus, any game played on a cribbage board must be a multiple of 60, plus 1. Indeed, when dominoes became popular in English pubs, the same board was adopted and it was subsequently passed on to darts. In the 1930s 'Domino!' was recorded as being one of the exclamations when a player won a game of darts.

Adopting the same principles as cribbage, the basic rule of darts became 'five times round' the board (a total of 300 points: 60 holes × 5, plus 1 for 'home': 301. By scoring a darts match on a cribbage board, players could check their score throughout the game. As darts evolved, proper scoreboards were introduced, usually a small blackboard on which to write the scores with a piece of chalk, making the cribbage board redundant.

In essence, the introduction of the '-01' games prevented darts from becoming boring and possibly disappearing completely into that section of historical research that comprises discarded and abandoned pub games. The game became more complex than simply shooting for the highest score and it lasted considerably longer and became more competitive.

If the odd '1' had not been introduced via the cribbage board it would have meant the players would have stayed in the 20 segment of the dartboard all the time, whereas '-01' meant that each player had to move away from that segment at some stage in order to gain victory. The double finish required in all games of '-01' also demands more than the ability to score well.

A cribbage board. Originally meant to score the card game of the same name, the board was later used for scoring dominoes and then darts. (Illustration: Chris Barrell)

Playing 501

Before the start of each game of 501, that number is written at the top of the scoreboard and each player's name or initial(s), or the appropriate team names, are written immediately below on the left-hand side and the right-hand side of the scoreboard thus:

	501	
Colin		Lynda

To decide who throws first, the order is determined by each player in turn throwing one single dart at the bullseye. The player whose dart is closest to it throws first. Other methods include throwing for the bullseye with your 'wrong hand', that is the one you do not normally use to throw your darts, or simply tossing a coin.

It has been known, on rare occasions, in professional, televised darts play, for the highly confident player who wins 'nearest the bull', and is thus entitled to throw first, to hand over that advantage to his opponent. This is a purely psychological ploy but one that does not always work.

There is a distinct advantage for the player throwing first. If the two players' scores are more or less equal after each throw then the person who threw second will always be playing catch-up. The equivalent in lawn tennis is that the player serving second has to break the serve of their opponent who started the game. In darts in a similar position the player is said to need to 'take the darts' off the other competitor.

Once it has been decided which player is to throw first it is usual practice for each of the competitors to be allowed six 'warm-up' darts, effectively to settle them down in readiness for the match. The match may then begin.

In most games of 501 the player goes 'straight in', which is to say that he or she begins scoring with their first scoring dart and does not have to achieve a starting double. The 'double in, double out' format established in the 1920s was phased out of the majority of standard matches in the 1970s, although some pockets of resistance to this change remain.

Each player throws three darts per turn, every score being recorded either by an official or, in more casual games, the next player waiting to play (this is called 'taking chalks') or, if no one else is around, the players themselves. The winner is the first player to complete their game by reducing the score of 501 to exactly zero; ensuring that the final dart hits the double required to do so.

Clearly, to win players must complete their game of 501 in the fewest number of darts. For this reason, most players using a standard dartboard concentrate on the 'red bit' or 'lipstick' – the treble 20. Three darts in that red segment scores the maximum possible of 180. (It is interesting to note that darts is the only target sport where the highest value segment is not the bullseye. Indeed, in addition to treble 20, treble 19 (57 points), treble 18 (54 points) and treble 17 (51 points) all exceed the score of the bullseye (50).)

However, hitting a 'maximum' or achieving other high-scoring totals does not guarantee you will win the game or the match. As twice World Championship runner-up Bobby George tells us: 'It's scoring for show, doubles for dough', by which he means it is no good being able to hit high-scoring trebles at will if you cannot then hit the double required to win the game. Therefore, players learning to play darts for the first time and wishing to succeed should practise hitting all segments of the dartboard: singles, doubles and trebles, high-scoring and low-scoring with equal intensity and application.

It is also one of the numerous skills of a good darts player to know their finish long before any winning double is in sight: more of which later.

After the player who won the right to throw first (in this example Lynda) has thrown her first three darts, the score is recorded and alongside it the balance left. Thus:

	501	
Lynda		Colin
120	381	

Lynda's opponent (Colin) then throws his three darts, which are similarly recorded:

	501		
Lynda		Colin	
120	381	85	416

The scoring continues in this way each throwing three darts in turn until the match is won. Thus, a completed scoreboard at the end of this sample game of 501 might look as follows:

	501		
Lynda		Colin	
120	381	85	416
100	281	80	336
83	198	100	236
75	123	26	210
91	32	14	196

The legend 'game shot' is rarely written on the scoreboard but is usually called by the scorer/chalker. Its inclusion here is purely by way of illustration to show that Lynda, by far the better player on this occasion, shot out on 32, probably finishing on double 16. As we can see, both Lynda and Colin scored well with their first nine darts but after that Lynda was by far the more consistent scorer and, not only that, was also able to take out the winning double quickly: with Colin way back on 196.

If these two players play a second game, who throws first? In friendly games it is usually a case of 'mug's away', an expression introduced to darts many years ago meaning the loser (whether it be Lynda or Colin) throws first in the next game every time. In more formal matches and league and tournament play, players throw alternately whatever the outcome of the previous game.

The 'Bust' Rule

In the majority of darts leagues and competitions, if a player scores more than is actually required, thereby 'busting' (also sometimes called 'bursting' their score), the player reverts back to the score he or she had before they threw any of their darts. As an example, let us say a player requires 24 (double 12) to win the game. He throws his first dart but, as he is having an off day, hits treble 12 (36 points). The score he needed has been exceeded and, in darts terminology, he has 'bust'. His turn is at an end and his remaining total reverts to 24.

In the early days of darts play before, and indeed for some time after, formal rules were drawn up, some local rules determined that players could revert to the score achieved by their last scoring dart. In the example above it is quite clear; the total needed had been exceeded by the very first scoring dart so the player reverted to requiring 24. But what would be the case if the score of 24 had been exceeded by the second or even the third dart? Let us return to the player requiring 24.

Needing 24 points to win the game, the player misses the double 12 with his first dart and instead hits a single 12, leaving a score of 12 (double 6). He then misses the double 6 with his second dart, which lands 'next door' in double 10, leaving 2 (double 1). His third dart misses double 1 by a fraction of an inch and unfortunately lands in double 20 (value 40 points). Therefore he has 'bust' his score. Under the 'last scoring dart' rule, the player does not revert to 24 points (the score he needed at the start of his turn) but to 2 points because his first two darts are deemed under this rule to have counted for score.

Although the majority of darts matches are nowadays played to standard rules, if you are new to an area and go to the pub or club, always check if any local rules apply. The BDO rule 11.03 states:

The 'Bust' rules shall apply, i.e. if a player scores more than the number required then that score shall not count, and the player's score shall revert back to the score the player required prior to the opponent's last throw.

In some cases, 'busting' is employed as a tactical move. For example, a player has left his favourite double, double 20 (40 points) but misses, hitting a single 20, which leaves 20 points (double 10). With his second dart, while going for double 10, he accidentally hits a single 15. This leaves 5 'to split', which means the player needs to hit an odd number (in this case a single 1 or a single 3) to bring the odd number back to an achievable even number. However, at this point, the player may choose to throw for a number larger than four and thus 'bust' the score so he goes back to his favourite double 20 on his next turn.

Any time a player is left with a score of 1 or zero (when not acquired by a winning double), that player has 'busted'.

The Importance of Knowing the Numbers

Before anyone can be proficient at the sport of darts it is vital to understand not only the position of each number, single, double and treble segment on the dartboard but also the value of those individual numbers and combinations. Even though darts can be played for fun, anyone wishing to achieve more would experience difficulties in playing and enjoying the game without this basic knowledge.

In 1968, darts player, coach and author, Noel E Williamson devised a singles, doubles and trebles combination chart. The chart, reproduced here with the permission of Noel's family, indicates not only the value of the double of each number but also all combinations from single, double or one treble to the maximum scores for each number, three trebles.

The only scoring areas of the dartboard not included in the chart are the outer bull (which only ever scores 25 points) and the bullseye (50 points). It should be noted the bullseye is also counted as double 25 so it can be used as a finishing double if a score of 50 remains to win the game.

Once a player is totally familiar with the values and positions of each of the numbers from 1 to 20 and their combinations, plus the outer bull and bullseye, they can begin to learn the more complex skill of calculating the 'outshots'; that is any shot comprising up to three darts in any one turn that ends with the winning double being hit.

Achieving the Outshot

A game of 501, or any '-01' game for that matter, can be completed in hundreds of different ways but, in the main, every player develops their own favourite way of finishing. Double 16 is a particularly popular outshot because if the player hits a single 16 instead, that leaves 16 (double 8) and if you *miss* that by hitting a single 8 that leaves 8 (double 4) and so on to 2 (double 1). It is important for everyone, especially novices and those hoping to improve their finishing, to learn some of the best ways to complete a game in both two and three darts.

To help you learn some of the outshots on a standard dartboard, an 'outshot chart' is reproduced here courtesy of David King of Darts501. com. The outshots shown are only a fragment of the number of the possible two and three-dart permutations of each number. Memorizing the outshots most appropriate to your own style of play early on is important but it is also likely as you gain experience you will develop others of your own with which you may feel more comfortable. Eventually, the outshots will become second nature to you and the chart will be discarded.

SINGLES, DOUBLES AND TREBLES COMBINATION CHART

Single	Double	Single & Double or one Treble	Two Doubles, or Single & Treble	Single & two Doubles, and Treble and two Singles or or Treble & Double	Single, Double and Treble, or two Trebles	Two Trebles and Single or Treble & two Doubles	Two Trebles & Doubles	Three Trebles (Maximum)
1	2	3	4	5	6	7	8	9
2	4	6	8	10	12	14	16	18
3	6	9	12	15	18	21	24	27
4	8	12	16	20	24	28	32	36
5	10	15	20	25	30	35	40	45
6	12	18	24	30	36	42	48	54
7	14	21	28	35	42	49	56	63
8	16	24	32	40	48	56	64	72
9	18	27	36	45	54	63	72	81
10	20	30	40	50	60	70	80	90
11	22	33	44	55	66	77	88	99
12	24	36	48	60	72	84	96	108
13	26	39	52	65	78	91	104	117
14	28	42	56	70	84	98	112	126
15	30	45	60	75	90	105	120	135
16	32	48	64	80	96	112	128	144
17	34	51	68	85	102	119	136	153
18	36	54	72	90	108	126	144	162
19	38	57	76	95	114	133	152	171
20	40	60	80	100	120	140	160	180

A singles, doubles and trebles combination chart. (Photo: Noel E. Williamson)

The highest outshot achievable in three darts is 170 (treble 20, treble 20 and bullseye). However, in my view, the most spectacular outshot, which harks back to the halcyon days of medieval archery when the best score was the centre of the target, is finishing a game on three bullseyes (150 points), the bullseye of course counting as 50 points or double 25.

There are a number of other ways to finish a game on 150, regarded by the experts as 'easier.' These include treble 20 (60 points), treble 20 (60 points) and double 15 (30 points) and double 20 (40 points), treble 20 (60 points) and bullseye (50 points).

The Bogey Numbers

There are seven scores under 170 that are described as 'bogey numbers' as there is no outshot possible with three darts. These numbers are 169, 168, 166, 165, 163, 162 and 159. As a player, you must remember them as to leave yourself any of those numbers may result in you handing the advantage to your opponent.

For those players who have yet to progress to thinking about three-dart outshots and look instead for a two-dart finish, you will learn that every number under 101, except one, is achievable in two darts. The exception, the bogey

number, is 99. If you do leave that number with your first dart it is impossible for you to finish the game with your remaining two darts. If you know that the score you have left is a manageable outshot, you must mentally check before you throw your first dart

OPPOSITE: A chart showing the most popular outshots from 170. (Image: David King/Darts 501. com)

Darts501.com — A Darts site for all Dart enthusiasts!

Three Dart Finishes

Score	1st Dart	2nd Dart	3rd Dart
170	T20	T20	Bull
169	--- No out shot---		
168	--- No out shot---		
167	T20	T19	Bull
166	--- No out shot---		
165	--- No out shot---		
164	T20	T18	Bull
163	--- No out shot---		
162	--- No out shot---		
161	T20	T17	Bull
160	T20	T20	D20
159	--- No out shot---		
158	T20	T20	D19
157	T20	T19	D20
156	T20	T20	D18
155	T20	T19	D19
154	T20	T18	D20
153	T20	T19	D18
152	T20	T20	D16
151	T20	T17	D20
150	T20	T18	D18
149	T20	T19	D16
148	T20	T16	D20
147	T20	T17	D18
146	T20	T18	D16
145	T20	T15	D20
144	T20	T20	D12
143	T20	T17	D16
142	T20	T14	D20
141	T20	T19	D12
140	T20	T16	D16
139	T19	T14	D20
138	T20	T18	D12
137	T19	T16	D16
136	T20	T20	D8
135	T20	T17	D12
134	T20	T14	D16
133	T20	T19	D8
132	T20	T16	D12
131	T20	T13	D16

Three Dart Finishes

Score	1st Dart	2nd Dart	3rd Dart
130	T20	20	Bull
129	T19	T16	D12
128	T18	T14	D16
127	T20	T17	D8
126	T19	T19	D6
125	25	T20	D20
124	T20	T16	D8
123	T19	T16	D9
122	T18	T20	D4
121	T17	T10	D20
120	T20	20	D20
119	T19	T10	D16
118	T20	18	D20
117	T20	17	D20
116	T20	16	D20
115	T20	15	D20
114	T20	14	D20
113	T20	13	D20
112	T20	12	D20
111	T20	19	D16
110	T20	18	D16
109	T19	20	D16
108	T20	16	D16
107	T19	18	D16
106	T20	14	D16
105	T19	16	D16
104	T18	18	D16
103	T20	3	D20
102	T20	10	D16
101	T20	1	D20
99	T19	10	D16

'501' game can be completed in 9 Darts
---180,180,141---
For FUN try this combination!
T20,T19, BULL (THREE TIMES!)
www.Darts501.com

Two Dart Finishes

Score	1st Dart	2nd Dart
100	T20	D20
98	T20	D19
97	T19	D20
96	T20	D18
95	T19	D19
94	T18	D20
93	T19	D18
92	T20	D16
91	T17	D20
90	T20	D15
89	T19	D16
88	T16	D20
87	T17	D18
86	T18	D16
85	T15	D20
84	T20	D12
83	T17	D16
82	T14	D20
81	T19	D12
80	T20	D10
79	T13	D20
78	T18	D12
77	T19	D10
76	T20	D8
75	T17	D12
74	T14	D16
73	T19	D8
72	T16	D12
71	T13	D16
70	T10	D20
69	T15	D12
68	T20	D4
67	T17	D8
66	T10	D18
65	T19	D4
64	T16	D8
63	T13	D12
62	T10	D16
61	T15	D8
60	20	D20

what score you must not achieve that would leave you on 99. In years gone by, leaving that number gave rise to the saying '99 never won a game'.

So use the checkout chart, learn the possible finishes and remember those bogey numbers. Also think through what is left if you miss your intended target(s). Pausing to think and recalculate interrupts your throwing action and the rhythm of your play and could cost you dearly.

The Perfect Nine-Dart 501

To finish any game of 501 in between eighteen and twenty-one darts is considered very good and ten to seventeen darts is top class but 'the dart player's Nirvana', the best you can achieve is the perfect nine-dart game. After only three visits to the oche the game is won. Many have compared this achievement in darts to scoring a 147 break in snooker.

Although there are many ways in which to achieve the perfect game, one of the most popular sequences comprises a player hitting six successive treble 20s (six darts: 360 points), which leaves 141, and then finishing the game by hitting another treble 20 (60 points), treble 19 (57 points) and double 12 (24 points and game shot).

On 13 October 1984, Derbyshire and England's John Lowe achieved the first televised, and the most celebrated, nine-dart perfect game at the MFI World Matchplay Championship in Slough. Lowe hit six successive treble 20s (360 points) and then finished the game with treble 17 (51 points), treble 18 (54 points) and double 18 (36 points and game shot). For this achievement, Lowe earned a financial bonus of £102,000, a staggering amount of money in those days. Lowe described the feat as 'two-and-a-half minutes of magic'.

As an aside, Lowe also won the tournament and received £12,000. He also received a cash prize for the highest outshot (£1,000), bringing his weekend's earnings to a massive £115,000, then a record payday for any darts player and a record that stood for many years.

Back in the 1980s, perfect games of 501 were rare but not now. With the growth of the professional game and the number of professional players, achieving a nine-dart 501 is a regular occurrence in major tournaments, especially those held under the PDC code. As a result, the financial rewards for doing so have dwindled. However, for the player new to darts or those looking to improve their game, a perfect nine-dart 501 remains their darting Nirvana.

CHAPTER 6

HOW TO IMPROVE YOUR SKILLS

Now you are aware of how to embrace the basics of the sport of darts you can begin to play and enjoy the game, learning from your friends and other opponents and by watching how they play, especially the more successful of them.

There is absolutely no reason why you should not discuss technique with other players. In fact you may well find that advice on how to improve your game is offered freely by those you play with and against.

While regular practice is the best way of becoming a better player, the advice contained in this chapter will help you develop your skills. It focuses on the mathematics of darts (knowledge of the dartboard and counting skills) and teaches you to prepare yourself for a darts match and where best to practise. Finally you will learn some general practice methods before moving on to Chapter 7, where I will suggest ways in which you can make this even more interesting.

The Mathematics of Darts

As you will have realised already, the standard dartboard is a complex target so it is an elementary fact that you must familiarize yourself with every segment and its value. Look at the dartboard illustrated here. This is the one that will usually face you when you step up to the oche, so learn the position of every numbered segment. From the top of the dartboard these read clockwise 20, 1, 18, 4, 13, 6, 10, 15, 2, 17, 3, 19, 7, 16, 8, 11, 14, 9, 12 and 5.

Darts requires the key skill of mental arithmetic.

Wait!

Please do not let 'maths' put you off. I am talking here about basic arithmetic addition, subtraction and multiplication. Clearly you need to be able to add up the scores obtained by each of your darts and to subtract that score from the total you have remaining, and to do so in double-quick time. Subtraction is very important as each dart reduces your score and you need to know instinctively and immediately what score is left. Multiplication is required as you need to know the value of each double and treble of every number. When you have mastered the basics of addition, subtraction and multiplication in darts you are a good way towards becoming a very competent player.

In the usual game of 501 discussed in the previous chapter, the aim is to work your way down to finishing on the appropriate double that reduces your total to exactly zero. Darts is not all about hitting high scores. It is most of all about finishing. As your score reduces, always look out for potential outshots, which you have already read about in Chapter 5.

But not all darts games run as smoothly as you might hope. What happens if your dart does not hit your intended target? You should have sufficient knowledge of the positions and values of all of the numbers and know what to do to resolve the problem. If you have to pause to stand and think what is actually required this will

A timely reminder of what a standard bristle dartboard looks like. (Photo: WINMAU Dartboard Co. Ltd)

undoubtedly break your rhythm and concentration, which could well cost you the match. Experience and time will make it possible for you to make split-second adjustments to your game.

Part of this learning process is also to be aware of what happens if you miss your required double and how to respond to it. If, for example, you need a score of 20 to finish the game you would normally go for double 10. But what should you do if you miss that double and hit a single 10? Clearly, this leaves 10 points (double 5) but where is that on the dartboard? Is it to the left of the 20 segment or the right? If you then miss the double 5, the dart landing in a single 5, what is your next target? Either a single 1 or a single 3, which would leave you double 2 or double 1 in your next throw.

Having memorized the position and value of each segment (single, double and treble) of the dartboard, you must be aware of how each double breaks down; thus ensuring you can adjust your throw if the intended target double, single or treble is missed.

Think about where you would go next if, when targeting 20 (double 10) you go wide of the mark with your first dart, hitting either a single 15 or a treble 6. What adjustment would you make to enable you to finish the game with your two remaining darts?

Most darts players eventually declare to having a favourite double, the one that they prefer to end each game with. As you have learned already, many players prefer to leave double 16 (32 points) because this is the only double on the dartboard that breaks down evenly no less than four times. But, of course, this only happens if you hit a single of the number you are aiming for. For example, if you miss the double 16 and hit a single 16 that will leave 16 points, which is double 8 right next door. However, hit a single 8 and that leaves 24 points, which means your attention, and your aim, moves to double 12.

Double 16, the most popular finishing double. (Photo: Tip Top Pics Ltd)

Worse still, if you hit a single 7 with your first dart, that will leave you an odd number (25 points). You will then have to use one of your remaining two darts to rectify the situation and bring you back to a double finish. In this particular example, many players would immediately adjust and go for a single 9, which would leave 16 points (double 8). There are, of course, many other single odd numbers you could aim for to 'take the odd off' and leave a double in addition to a single 9: these being 17, 15, 13, 11, 7, 5, 3 or 1 but single 9, double 8 tends to be the most popular. You must always be prepared to adjust to the effect on your game of the errant dart.

If you miss the double 16 completely with your first dart and then hit a single 7 with your second, all you can do with the remaining dart is bring your score down

to a manageable double. In this example, you may have handed over the advantage to your opponent, who may be ready and waiting to finish the game. Only if he or she misses with their next three darts will you be once again in a position to win. So many games are lost due to missing doubles.

A good number of professional darts players like to finish their games on double top (double 20, 40 points) because this is the second highest scoring double (the highest being the bullseye). That's fine, although players new to the game should note that double 20 (40 points) breaks down into double 10 (20 points) then double 5 and, if you narrowly miss that, to single 5. However, it is likely that a good opponent would have finished the game before you reached that point.

Learning the mathematics of darts is crucial and in time will become second nature to you. The chances are that very soon you will be planning your games mentally as you go along so you leave your favourite *winning* double, whatever that may be.

How to Prepare for a Game

Good preparation for any game is key and comprises four elements: preparation of your body, mind, appearance and darts equipment.

How do you prepare for any important familiar task?

You organize yourself properly by establishing a routine (not a ritual). So it is with darts. Before a match you must check your equipment to ensure your darts, flights and shafts are in good order. You should also make sure a spare set of similar darts and accessories are available just in case damage occurs during a game or your darts are lost or mislaid. If you are in any doubt whatsoever about the safety of your darts then leave the spare set and replacement flights and shafts with a trusted friend who is standing by.

In tournament matches, to ensure peace of mind, you must be fully aware of what arrangements need to be in place, exactly where the venue is, what time you need to be there to register and, of course, how you are travelling there: car, taxi, bus, train or walking. (Professional players will have managers or personal aides that take care of such matters and thus relieve the pressure on them.)

Go through your upcoming game in your mind and make sure you are prepared mentally for the challenge and ready to play the best game you possibly can.

You should not underestimate the importance of practising at home before you leave for a match. I recommend you undertake some warm-up exercises without your darts, such as arm swings and body stretches, anything that loosens the arm, hands and legs that will help prepare you physically for the game. Practise again at the venue. Even in pub and club matches, time is given for players to 'warm up' before the darts proper begin. This also helps you acclimatize to your surroundings.

At local level, players are not on the oche for very long but in major tournaments some matches may take two hours to complete. If you are a local pub or club player who just walks in hoping to play a game of darts, you might not think that any preparation is necessary. But whatever your level it is vital, whether you play for fun, league points or money. You should never play 'cold'.

At all levels of play, ensure you prepare yourself for each and every game. That way you will be best placed to perform well and give of your very best – win or lose.

Where to Practise

If you are lucky enough to have a proper darts set-up at home then you can, within the restrictions of your day job, family responsibilities and so on, practise for as many hours as you like to hone your skills. However, despite playing well in the privacy of their own home practice environment, some players find it difficult to transfer the quality of their practice play to the competitive oche. Many find that they play excellent darts in the practice room or on the practice boards at the venue yet fail to produce that same quality of darts play when they toe the oche and the pressure is on.

On many occasions, a player who has just lost a match says something like: 'I don't know what went wrong. I was playing great in practice.' Usually the reason why a player loses a game they should have won is to do with the player being unable to adapt themselves to what to them is probably outside their comfort zone. Therefore it is necessary to learn those skills that will enable you to play good darts anywhere, even at a venue you might initially perceive as being an alien environment.

Let us have a look at some of the other skills you need to acquire to enable you to deal with this.

Practice, Practice, Practice and More Practice

Although this has already been mentioned, probably more than once, there is nothing that will help you improve more than regular, well-constructed and organized practice. It is the only way to succeed in any sport.

To derive the most benefit from practising, you should set aside specific amounts of time on specific days, those best suited to you and your lifestyle, and then stick to that pattern as much as you can. Approach practice in a well-structured way.

Most casual darts players practise when they can, while the more serious of such players might be at the dartboard for half an hour or an hour every day. More serious players might look to schedule three, four or even more hours each day.

Many casual players do not practise at all but then, in the main, they are not bothered about developing their game over and above what they can achieve on the night, preferring more to play and enjoy the social aspect above everything else.

For those wishing to play serious darts and perhaps even turn professional, they will never succeed to the top flight of the sport unless they count their practice sessions in hours rather than minutes. To properly enjoy winning at darts regular, dedicated practice is essential.

Another way of ensuring improvement is to play in your local pub or club against players you regard, for the moment at least, to be better than you. That way you can gauge your progress, improve your game and, over time, as you take a game or two off them, your self-confidence.

If you have taken practice seriously then your regime will not just consist of throwing at specific numbers and segments, such as the treble 20 bed. You will have varied the areas on which to concentrate. You must become proficient in hitting every scoring area of the dartboard but, to prevent boredom setting in, you must make every effort to make practice interesting. This will undoubtedly lead to improvement.

I suggest you begin by writing the numbers 1 to 20 on a piece of paper down the page. Then approach the oche, adopt your stance and throw three darts at each of the numbers in numerical order, recording as you go along the number of darts it takes to hit each number once. It does not matter at this stage whether you hit a single, a double or a treble. Hitting the correct segment is all-important.

When you reach the stage of being able, consistently, to hit the segments 1 to 20 in 25 darts or fewer then you should move on to going round the dartboard in numerical order on doubles. Doubles are much more difficult to hit as they are so much smaller than the part of the segment that scores a single of each number. However, practice on doubles is vital in darts as the double always concludes standard games. The winning shot is always a double but not always your favourite, preferred double, so practise them all.

Remember too that in some areas games are still started by a double in.

Once you have mastered the doubles, you can move on to the trebles (again round the dartboard in as few darts as possible) and then finally turn your attention to the bullseye and the outer bull.

Early on you may discover your ability to finish games is impaired by inexperience and so you may well find yourself occasionally in the 'madhouse'; only 2 points left, double 1. But do not be afraid of this number. You have no further to go, so go for it. In fact, do not be afraid of any double, any treble or any single

England international Deta Hedman. (Photo: Tip Top Pics Ltd)

John Lowe focuses on the target. (Photo: Tip Top Pics Ltd.)

number. They are all the same distance away from you as you stand at the oche, so hitting double 1 should hold no more fear for you than if you were going for your favourite double.

Concentration

Wherever you choose to play darts, you are bound to experience distractions of one kind or another. These could take the form of general noise within the pub or venue, shouts from supporters or teammates or the actions of your opponent trying to put you off your game.

You must learn to deal with these interruptions in a professional and confident way otherwise, whatever the distraction is, it will directly affect your ability to concentrate on the game in hand. Distractions that cannot be dealt with immediately will lead to tension, poor performance and, inevitably, lost games and matches.

While standing at the oche, you must be fully focused on your game. Nothing else. Only then will you produce the goods, namely your best darts. So, when you step up to the oche, blank out all distractions otherwise you will never be in control of your own game. Expect both the expected (for example, shouts from the opponents' team while you are taking your throw) and the unexpected (say, a tray of

Phil 'The Power' Taylor exudes confidence in a match against Cheshire's Dave Chisnal. (Photo: Tip Top Pics Ltd)

drinks sent accidentally crashing to the floor). Prepare yourself mentally for each and every game. If your concentration is at its best, even if you do not win the match you will know that you have given of your best.

Although some may deny it, losing does hurt. No one likes to come second. Analyze the game afterwards and decide what went wrong and what actions you need to take to correct it for next time.

That known, return to your practice board.

Confidence

In addition to mastering the basic skills of playing darts, self-confidence and self-belief are vitally important parts of your darting skills arsenal.

When playing a player whom you

know has been more successful than you in the past, do not stand in awe of him or her. Do not shy away from or be affected by the reputation of any opponent. This is self-defeating. Always, always play the best game you are able. Be ready. Be focused. Remember, in essence, darts is you against the dartboard.

Stay confident throughout the game or match. Do not send out any signals

Dutch player Jimmy Hendriks holds his head in his hands after missing a crucial double. (Photo: Tip Top Pics Ltd)

to your opponent that might tell him or her you are having a bad day. Do not drop your head after an isolated poor shot or a missed double. Do not give yourself a 'team talk' within his or her hearing.

External signs of distress may encourage your opponent to play even better, spurred on by your obvious display of disappointment following an errant dart. Keep focused. If you lose a leg of a match, fight back in the next. Refuse to lie down. While the match can still be won, never give up. At all times remain confident.

Nerves

Allied to self-confidence is the defeating of any cause of nervousness. It is not unusual

Kent and England legend Tony Brown takes a drink during competition back in the days when drinking alcohol was allowed on stage at tournaments. (Photo: Author's Darts Archive)

Virtually unbeatable for more than two decades Phil Taylor's reputation went before him, often beating opposition players before a dart was thrown. (Photo: Tip Top Pics Ltd)

Another visit to the toilet is made. In extreme cases (but rarely at a local level) a player might feel physically sick. Thus, the chances are that even before a dart is thrown, you stand a defeated player.

Nerves have a direct impact on your performance; crucial trebles and potentially winning doubles are missed. The problem or problems need to be addressed. However, while not wishing to dig deep into medical solutions or complex academic or psychological theory, it is important for the player to recognize and admit a problem exists. Once that is accepted, you must deal with the problem using the method best suited to your individual condition.

Drinking does not help. It only exacerbates your problems. It is not about seeking out some quirky medical solution. It is more about coming to terms with your problems, dealing with them the best you can and having confidence in your own skills. It is about achieving the correct mindset that will enable you to step up to any oche and throw your darts in a confident and stress-free manner.

Talking to friends might help but there are self-help DVDs, CDs and internet websites and downloads that may assist you. That said, take great care to analyze exactly where the problems lie. I believe the majority of causes of stress can then be resolved by learning to relax. Relax and focus on what you know, which is that you are a competent and confident darts player.

Reputations

At whatever level of darts you play, there will always be a small number of players whose reputation as a good or great player precedes him or her.

At the highest level, a player with a formidable reputation already has a psychological advantage over their opponent *provided* the opponent lets it affect them and their game.

for players to be nervous before a big match. Nerves, primarily tension or stress, can affect directly your performance on the oche and are manifested in any number of physical or mental forms.

For no apparent reason, you may begin to doubt your own skills. All of a sudden you convince yourself you are not good enough. You begin fidgeting with your darts or your hands shake.

Fans at a PDC Premier League match fill the venue to capacity. (Photo: Tip Top Pics Ltd)

Young women eagerly await their heroes. (Photo: Tip Top Pics Ltd)

If you ever find yourself in this position, take it all in your stride, concentrate and play your best game. You may even raise your game and you might even win.

Onlookers

Onlookers could just be your friends at the pub or club, your teammates and the opposition on a match night or, at the highest level, thousands of fans in a huge auditorium. If you are going to play darts at a competitive level then you need to be able to deal with this.

Yorkshire's John Walton celebrates winning the 2001 BDO World Championships with trophy and lucky teddy. (Photo: Steve Daszko)

Double World Champion Adrian Lewis brings referee Russ Bray's attention to an incident in 2012 during his match with Wales' Ritchie Burnett. (Photo: Tip Top Pics Ltd)

People watching you play will always be supporting their team or favourite player. It is not uncommon for people to heckle a player while he or she is throwing, even at the highest level. Pleas from the referee often work but the crowd can never be policed totally, so players must prepare themselves for such distractions.

Some players achieve this by playing loud music while they practise on the basis that if they can play a great game accompanied by that cacophony of sound then they can produce the same great game in front of a noisy crowd.

Rituals

One of the causes of nerves and resultant poor darts play can be when rituals go wrong.

Many darts players go through some kind of ritual before a match. These might include walking to the venue via the same route every time and avoiding the cracks in the pavement or wearing their favourite 'lucky' socks or underwear. Then, of course, there are the darts you have always used, those lucky flights and that lucky charm you *must* wear around your neck.

The purpose of such rituals is supposedly to bring good fortune, instil confidence in the player and form an important part of the final preparation for a game. But what happens if something goes wrong? You forget your lucky socks. You lose your darts. Such events can be psychologically damaging and it is inevitable your level of performance on the oche will deteriorate, while inside your head your final preparation has been incomplete.

Avoid such rituals.

The best case scenario for beginners is simple. Do not engage in any rituals whatsoever. But, for those already engaging in such things, only willpower and your own determination to free yourself from

the bond of the ritual will overcome the existing condition, the hold that established ritual holds over you and your ability to play well.

Anger

There is no place for anger on the oche.

Anger, demonstrated by throwing a dart or darts as hard as you can at the dartboard, is not only unsportsmanlike but is also potentially dangerous. Such action can cause darts to bounce off the board. Anger does not control the direction of the dart, which could end up anywhere.

Tempers must be controlled so as not to put your opponent, the chalker, bystanders or indeed yourself, in harm's way.

Gamesmanship

The dictionary definition of gamesmanship is 'skill in using ploys to gain a victory or advantage over another person'. Basically, in sport it is the art of putting your opponent off.

English author Stephen Potter subtitled his book Gamesmanship (1947) 'The art of winning games without actually cheating'. Surprisingly perhaps, Potter applied his 'art' to darts, his advice including that you: 'Question your darts opponent closely on the exact area of the dart where he deems it wisest to exert maximum thumb-and-finger pressure.'

Back in the supposedly 'good old days', when smoking was allowed during darts matches at all levels of play, those who smoked were sometimes tempted to (or actually did) puff smoke across the sightline of their opponent, the purpose being of course to merely distract him or her or, more likely, to impair their vision – or both.

Even with that tactic now consigned to history in the UK by the smoking ban in pubs and other public places, there remain other acts of

gamesmanship available to the more disreputable opponent, so be on your guard.

Among the tactics employed by such darting ne'er do wells are, as you are about to throw, standing behind you and clicking their darts together, talking to themselves (but within earshot), talking to you ('Oh. Good shot!'), shuffling their feet, clinking their water jug and glass, playing with small change in their pocket, clearing their throat at opportune moments (usually when you are about to throw), coughing, whistling and even other natural noises that need not be expanded upon here. They will do anything to distract you and break your concentration.

In any darts tournament at any level the referee's or official's attention should be drawn to any incident of this kind if he or she has not already realised what is going on. But over and above any of these wily manoeuvres of gamesmanship there is one that is allowed as it is not breaking any specific rule: the art of slowing down the speed of the game. This is achieved primarily by one of the players throwing their darts at a slower speed than would normally be expected and then taking just a little more time to remove their darts from the board before returning to their position standing the approved distance behind their opponent. Slowing down a game can directly affect an opponent's rhythm and concentration, which then leads to them making mistakes.

The opposite, naturally, is speeding the game up by throwing your darts faster than your opponent in a bid to unsettle him or her by pressing them to throw quicker than they would normally do.

Multi-World Champion Stoke-on-Trent's Phil 'The Power' Taylor, when asked about acts of gamesmanship in the professional sport of darts, commented: 'If you are practising gamesmanship, you cannot be fully concentrating on your own game.'

Back on the pub oche, in friendly

England's Adrian Lewis and Wales' Ritchie Burnett in dispute during a tournament in 2012. (Photo: Tip Top Pics Ltd)

games rather than organized league matches, gamesmanship is often seen as part of the fun of playing casual darts. Each player is expected to give as good as he or she gets.

Making running repairs is a legitimate interruption. The game is temporarily halted while a player replaces a damaged flight or a broken shaft. This is also on occasions used to stop the match deliberately for a short while, while the opponent mentally regroups.

Once all interruptions have been overcome, you may find yourself poised to win the game, set or even the match. Do not be in a hurry to finish your opponent off. Keep calm. A good number of players do become stressed as the conclusion of a leg, a game or match is within their grasp.

Even the top professionals sometimes wilt under such pressure and miss winning opportunities. Maintain your concentration at all times. Let tension seep in and you could easily lose the game. Think of that winning double as you would any other target, any other segment on the dartboard; numbers and segments you have practised long and hard to make your own.

In any event, responsible players everywhere at whatever level can prepare themselves physically and mentally for each game and learn how to deal with gamesmanship or any other interruption, whether it be from the opponent or those watching.

Having now prepared yourself for all eventualities and you have started to become a confident and skilled player, it is now time to see how we can make your regular practice more enjoyable.

CHAPTER 7

MAKING YOUR PRACTICE INTERESTING

It is a recognized fact that practice can be dull. It can be boring. It is up to you to make it interesting otherwise the chances are your growing passion for darts will begin to diminish as you do not make the progress you expect.

A footballer would not just practise taking penalties and a golfer does not restrict her or his practising to putting, so why should a darts player only practise on the 20 segment?

While you have familiarized yourself with every segment of the dartboard and learned the outshots, what follows are a few games that can be played either with or without a practice partner that will bring variety to your training regime, or quite simply, are fun to play while you continue to learn and hone your skills.

Towards the end of this section, I will include practice advice from four professional darts players, three-time World Darts Champion John Lowe; the 1988 Embassy World Darts Champion and three-time WINMAU World Master Bob Anderson; Leicester's Jamie Caven, at the time of writing an up-and-coming player in the Top 25 of the Professional Darts Corporation's Order of Merit; and 1983 World Darts Champion Keith Deller.

But let's ease into this…

High Twelve

For the beginner, the game of High Twelve focuses on the 20-segment where the highest scores are to be found. Treble 20 is the highest scoring segment on a standard dartboard and three trebles 20s attained in one throw of three darts comprises the maximum score possible – 180.

This game is a gentle introduction to organized practice, the aim being to

achieve the highest score you can with twelve darts, that is four throws of three darts each. Have a pencil and paper handy so that each total score from twelve darts can be recorded and you can measure your improvement from one practice session to the next. High Twelve can, of course, be played on any high-numbered segment so you eventually improve your accuracy on all the big numbers.

But, in darts, it is not always the high-scoring numbers you need to hit. Thus the aim of its companion game, Low Twelve, is to hit the lowest score you can with twelve darts. Start with the number 1 and then move on to the other low scoring segments.

Dr Darts' Round the Board

One of my practice games is my own version of going round the board. I throw three darts at each segment 1 to 20 in numerical order, counting singles, doubles and trebles as one point each. Thus, the most points that can be achieved is 60 (three out of three darts in each of the 20 segments).

As always, keep a record of your scores and the date you achieved them and take pride in your improving total.

Straight in 101

Find me on a Wednesday evening in my local, The Carpenters Arms, in Maldon, Essex, and I'll doubtless be playing 'first to ten' Straight in 101 with my best friend Colin Barrell. We play it for fun – loser buys (usually me).

Straight in 101 is ideal practice too and affords players the chance to shoot out in

The author at play, his favourite practice game being Straight in 101. (Photo: Darts Archive/David King, Darts501.com)

only two darts. In theory, there should be no need to chalk this game but, trust me, it is best to because it is not as easy as it looks. In your early days of playing Straight in 101 the game can take time.

You start with a score of 101 and, like a standard game, the task is to reduce your score to zero. If you are unable to achieve this in two darts (treble 17, bullseye) whatever you hit should still leave you a two-dart finish. For example, if you aim for treble 17 but hit a single 17, that leaves you 84, a score that can be achieved any number of ways, one example of which is treble 20 (60 points), double 12 (24 points and game).

There are, of course, many other ways to start the game but only treble 17, bullseye affords you the chance to hit the perfect game of 101. The *imperfect* game is when your first dart misses the treble 17 and hits a single 2. That leaves 99, the 'bogey number', which you already know is a score that cannot be finished in two darts, thereby letting your opponent in.

Playing Straight in 101 has a number of benefits, including improving your accuracy and your mental arithmetical skills.

John Lowe's recommended practice regime includes Ten Up. (Photo: Tip Top Pics Ltd)

When you reach a point where 101 is easy to hit, move on to 101 – Double In or Straight in 201.

Middle for Diddle

This game focuses your mind and your darts on the bullseye and the outer bull, and can be played on your own or with a playing partner. The aim is to reduce a score of 501 to zero but this is no ordinary game of 501.

Starting with *any* double on the dartboard (including the bullseye), each player scores only on bullseyes (50 points) and outer bullseyes (25 points). Nothing outside the outer bull counts at all. Carry on until you hit that game-winning double.

A slight variant is Straight in Middle for Diddle, where no starting double is required. While this, like the original version, is excellent practice for the bullseye and outer bull, your finishing double will *always* be double 13.

John Lowe's Ten Up

Three-time World Professional Darts Champion John Lowe has been advising players of all skill levels how to play the game for many years and recommends Ten Up as ideal practice on the treble 20. It is a straightforward practice game where you are only rewarded for scoring on that 'red bit'.

All darts must land in the 20 segment. Only scores of 100-plus count and each score must include one or more treble 20s. Thus, if you score three double 20s (a total score of 120 points) that score does not count!

For each treble 20 scored during

The 1988 Embassy World Professional Darts Champion, Bob Anderson practises using a game of his own invention Bob's 27. (Photo: Tip Top Pics Ltd)

each throw in a 100-plus score, award yourself one point. If you hit a treble 20 but your total score is 100, you score nothing. It must be 100-plus. A score of 140 with two treble 20s will score two points: 180. Three darts in the treble 20 scores three points.

The name of the game is Ten Up and that's what you have to achieve. Score ten points in the shortest time possible, remembering always your score must be over 100 and include at least one treble 20.

As always, keep a note of your score and the date so as to measure your progress.

Bob's 27s

While researching this book I also contacted the 1988 World Professional Darts Champion Bob Anderson, who told me: 'Patrick, practice should always keep your interest and not be boring. That's why I never practise just 501. I use a variety of practice,

Jamie 'Jabba' Caven, has become one of the top PDC players of recent times despite being diabetic and blind in one eye. (Photo: Tip Top Pics Ltd)

Keith Deller, the 1983 Embassy World Professional Darts Champion, shares his practice and warm-up regime. (Photo: Tip Top Pics Ltd)

including a game I invented many years ago called Bob's 27s. This game is a great little practice routine and concentrates on doubles accuracy. You can keep a note of the running score on paper, in your head or on your chalk board.

'You start off with 27 points and go round the board throwing three darts at each double, from double 1 to bull in sequence. Every double you hit earns you that doubles score and is added to your total, but missing a double with all three darts means you must subtract the value of that double from your total. Once you're down to zero or less, the game is over.'

Anderson's best ever score in Bob's

27s is 811, achieved 'a long time ago'. He added: 'I now regularly get in the 600s and consider that a very good score.'

Players new to the game should set their sights a little lower!

Jamie Caven's Practice Regime

Like Anderson, Caven told me it is vital to ensure practice is kept interesting. He said: 'If you become bored, you will lose interest quickly,' adding: 'My practice mainly consists of finishing.'

Here's an example of his practice regime.

He told me: 'I would probably have five or ten throws at the bull first to obtain my range. Then do three throws at 81 finish. If I hit single 19, then single 12 and miss the bull you go back to 81, so you have to check out each score as it stands. If you do it within three attempts you then go to 82. If you don't do it you go down to 80. The idea is to get to and finish 100.' Caven added: 'This game can be tailored so an amateur could start on 41 to 60 maybe.'

Caven's practice then continues by concentrating on scoring in the 20 segments only until he has scored at least 1,000 points.

Keith Deller's Warm-Up and Practice

The 1983 Embassy World Darts Champion told me: 'I found the best way to practise is to start off with a thirty-minute warm-up. Then, for two hours, practise finishing. Start at 80, then once you hit that go for 81 and keep doing that and see how close you get to 130.'

Deller added: 'Once your time has finished, write down how far you get and then try to beat it next time. The good thing is that you are practising all trebles. Phil Taylor used to practise that a lot.'

Rewards

I seem to recall, many years ago, a world snooker champion revealing that to encourage improvement while practising he prepared his favourite snack or non-alcoholic drink beforehand and left it within plain view on a shelf in close proximity to the snooker table.

He set himself a high target break or a set number of balls to pocket. As soon as he had achieved it he awarded himself the 'prize', always remembering to wash his hands after eating and before he started on his next practice session.

The same can apply to you. You must have a favourite snack or drink. Try it. But do not set the target too low. That would be tantamount to cheating!

Individual and Team Games

Whatever practice regime suits you there is absolutely no substitute, after you have mastered the basics, for playing darts one-against-one or as a member of a team. This is for real; a chance to apply the lessons, advice and skills you have learned from this book and to put your countless hours of practice to a proper test.

But do you need to be fit to be able to play darts well?

PART 3

DEVELOPING YOUR GAME

CHAPTER 8

HEALTH, FITNESS AND WELL-BEING

I am certain it is generally assumed that to play darts you do not need to be fit. That appears to be the popular perception. After all, what exercise or dietary regime do you need to sit in a pub or club, drinking and chatting and waiting for your name to be called either to chalk the next game or to play?

Exercise

To play any sport well you need to be fit. Some sports demand hour upon hour of exercise, toning the body and strict regimes. I am not suggesting you need to do that to be able to play darts well but you do need to do something to maintain a level of mental and physical fitness to enable you to concentrate and stay alert if you want to win. (See warnings on alcohol, smoking and drugs below.)

Nowadays, the majority of top players exercise regularly and many take to the golf links when not standing at the oche.

Disability

Darts is proud to be a sport that can be played by *anyone* regardless of gender, ability or disability. In recent years, great strides have been made by the World Disability Darts Association (WDDA), the brainchild of English-born Australian Russ Strobel, which is the end product of a campaign designed to open up darts to players with disabilities.

In 2010, equipment was designed by Strobel that enables wheelchair dart players to play on a par with able-bodied darters. The unique Wildfire 137 dart frame (pictured here) features both a dartboard set at the standard height and a lowered dartboard that enables a wheelchair player and a standing player to compete directly against each other at the same oche. Strobel says: 'The gentle physical movement of throwing and retrieving their own darts, combined with the exciting mental challenges, gives a comprehensively beneficial activity that can be played at almost any age.'

Strobel and his board of administrators (of which I am proud to be a member) have gained recognition from the World Darts Federation (WDF) not only for their achievements in respect of disabled players but also their product, the Wildfire 137. The WDF has also agreed the Wildfire 137 may be used in competition. The WDDA continues to promote equality in darts on a global basis. Strobel told me: 'It is a fun and supportive social network, and of all of the sports there are none that holds greater potential than darts to improve one's overall feeling of well-being long term.'

For more information, visit www.world-disability-darts.org

Russ Strobel, inventor of the Wildfire dart frames, with the Wildfire 137. (Photo: WDDA/Russ Strobel)

Alcohol and Cigarettes

Drinking alcohol does *not* make you a better player. After a few pints you may

Russ Strobel demonstrates the Solo dart frame. (Photo: WDDA/Russ Strobel)

Wheelchair Dartboard Height

Both rear wheels of wheelchair must be behind the throwing line

137cm from ground to centre of bullseye

237cm from board face to throwing line

Wheelchair darts set-up. (Illustration: David King/Darts501.com)

think it does but alcohol is a depressant. It cannot aid performance. Ignore all the stories you may have heard of (primarily) men boasting they play better after consuming large quantities of strong beer or lager.

Of course, beer has always been part of the culture of darts because the game was born of the English pub, where it lay relatively undisturbed in the public bar played by millions for decade upon decade. Then, in the 1970s men, and to a lesser extent women, found themselves thrust on to the small screen. Darts players, who had until then played only in their local pubs or clubs, in annual tournaments such as brewery league cups or, on a national scale, at the *News of the World* Individual Darts Championship, were fast becoming television sports stars.

The players' habits of drinking and smoking accompanied them on to the TV stage, which eventually became a world stage. Beer bellies, created by over-indulgence in beer or lager and late-night curries, Chinese meals and takeaways, were often seen so soon the adage became: 'You can take the darts out of the pub but not the pub out of the darts.' In other words, larger venues, be they halls or cabaret clubs, were seen merely as large pubs. However, drinking and smoking on stage were eventually banned by the darts organizations, the latter even before the Government ban was introduced.

The general rule as regards alcohol is, if you must drink, follow the Government guidelines. However, I understand how this can be challenging in a busy pub environment. So, if you enjoy a drink, try your best to do so in moderation.

Smoking in public places, such as pubs, shops, restaurants and clubs, has been outlawed in Scotland since 2006 and in England, Northern Ireland and Wales since 2007. Previously stuffy, smoke-filled pubs and clubs are now happily a thing of the past in the UK but the ban is not global.

Despite UK pubs and club oches being smoke free, everyone is aware of the risks they run if they smoke and the damage

Like many other players in the past, Eric Bristow would smoke on stage. (Photo: Harrows Darts)

they can cause to themselves and those around them. Smoking can directly affect your performance in any sport, even darts.

Diet

Eating too much or too little before a match can easily have an impact on the way you play, in the same way as a lack of exercise, excessive drinking or smoking.

Too much food can make you feel uncomfortable and while you are experiencing discomfort you cannot give your full attention to the game in hand. Too little food can also cause problems such as nausea.

Make certain you eat sensibly and appropriately for the sport you play. There is, of course, a temptation in darts to substitute alcohol for food. This is not recommended.

If necessary, seek specialist dietary advice.

Drugs

Organizations worldwide recognize that the use of performance-enhancing drugs in sport, *any* sport, is a massive problem.

It may seem unusual that darts should be included but it is a fact that random drug testing of players at the highest level has been introduced by both the British Darts Organisation (BDO) and the Darts Regulation Authority (DRA); the latter concerned with those players playing under the auspices of the Professional Darts Corporation (PDC).

Bizarrely, some might think, the definition of drugs in a darts context does not include alcohol. However, performing badly, being verbally abusive or physically violent on the oche, whether alcohol-fuelled or not, is covered under performance-related rules and regulations.

Dartitis

In 2007, the Oxford English Dictionary included the word 'dartitis' for the first time, defining the condition as 'a state of nervousness which prevents a player from releasing a dart at the right moment when throwing.'

The word had first appeared in *Darts World* magazine in 1981, coined by the then editor Tony Wood to describe a condition whereby a player finds himself or herself unable to release a dart (or darts) properly. The dart is picked up. The dart is brought up to eye level and the aim corrected. The dart is drawn back… and that's where it stays! (In this, dartitis is similar to the 'yips' in golf, where the player goes to swing the club but is unable to bring it down to complete the movement.)

Players who have suffered from this condition include the author and professional players Mark Walsh, a top PDC player, and, famously, the five-time World Professional Darts Champion Eric Bristow.

Although the problem of dartitis has been the subject of much research and discussion on darts forums and in magazines, there appears to be no single solution and thus opinions differ on not only the causes but the solutions.

For some, the solution is to change from a heavy dart to a lighter one or even changing the hand with which you throw a dart. Others claim it is psychological, that

Like Eric Bristow and others, PDC darts player Mark Walsh has also suffered from dartitis. (Photo: Tip Top Pics Ltd)

the cause is deeply imbedded in the psyche and say professional help is essential.

One serious pub player rid himself of dartitis by examining the potential causes. He eventually changed his throw (he took a deep breath before each throw and expelled the air with the throw) and threw his darts slower. He also improved his chances of overcoming the condition successfully by 'leaving any home and work worries outside'.

Although he was never able to revert to his world championship-winning level of play, Eric Bristow eventually cured his dartitis by going back to the style of throw he had used pre-1983. He also changed his diet, reducing his intake of junk food. I cured my dartitis by ceasing to drink strong lager and reverting to good old English real ale.

With such a variety of 'cures' for the condition known as 'dartitis', it is clear you must seek the solution that best suits your particular case. However, I suggest that if you are a sufferer, before you do anything else visit my website www.patrickchaplin. com/Dartitis.htm for guidance.

CHAPTER 9

OTHER ACCESSORIES

The most important darts accessories, the flight and shaft, need to be checked regularly and, if necessary, replaced. Installing a properly marked out darts mat and efficient lighting have also been mentioned previously. However, over and above these items and, of course, the darts and dartboard, there are many other products that are designed to assist or improve your game.

Limited space does not allow publication of anywhere near a full list of what is available, so what follows is but a small selection of what I regard as the most effective aids to efficiency and improvement. For those wishing to view the full extent of what the major darts companies can provide, website addresses are given in the Useful Contacts section.

Checkout Chart

The need to refer to a checkout chart in the early days of your play has already been mentioned but it is worth noting here the majority of darts companies produce pocket-sized versions. These cannot cover every checkout possibility but will feature what are considered to be the most popular two or three-dart finishes.

Do not be embarrassed to carry a checkout chart with you and refer to it from time to time. It is all part of the learning process. In less time than you think, the checkouts will come to you automatically and you will be able to discard the chart.

Darts Wallets and Cases

All sets of quality modern darts come complete with either a wallet made of leatherette or in a strong plastic or aluminium case, the purpose of which is to protect your darts and to fit neatly into your pocket or handbag.

There are many players who are not satisfied with a standard wallet or case and need something more impressive in which to store their darts and accessories. For them, a wide variety of alternatives are available, including cases that accommodate not only the player's darts, flights and shafts but also provide room for spare flights, stems or even a second set of darts. For fans of two-time Lakeside World Champion Ted Hankey, nicknamed The Count after his schoolboy obsession with Dracula and all things vampiric, a 'coffin case' is available!

Wallets and cases, while protecting your darts and accessories when not in use, cannot prevent those with light fingers walking off with your treasured arrows. Until such a thing as a 'darts alarm' is invented, please ensure you carry your wallet or case with you wherever you go or leave it in the care of someone you trust.

Darts Sharpeners

The points of all three of your darts need to be maintained to a high standard and thus they should be monitored on a regular basis to ensure they remain sharp. Blunt or damaged points can mean the difference between winning or losing a game, or even a tournament. If not maintained they might well bounce out of the dartboard or if they are unable to penetrate the board properly they may simply fall out.

In the past, points were kept sharp by using sandpaper or rubbing the points on a stone – or even the pub brickwork! Today the most common method is to use a simple darts

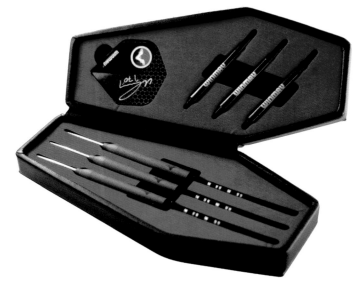

Ted Hankey's coffin case. (Photo: WINMAU Dartboard Co. Ltd)

sharpener where you insert the dart point and move it around in a circular motion to remove burrs and sharpen each point. As you can see from the photograph, this example is combined with a key ring that ensures if emergency on-the-spot repairs are required, the sharpener is always to hand.

One of the latest developments is a pen-sized sharpener made with a fine-coated diamond grit roughing surface. The action of moving the dart point up and down the coated rod sharpens each point very effectively.

Sharpeners are also available in wall-mounted electronic versions but these are more for installing in pubs and clubs than to be bought by individuals.

Eventually, there may come a time when the points have become extremely blunt and the point worn down by consistent wear and no amount of sharpening can help. Years of darting can take their toll. At this point, some players replace their darts completely. However, the majority of players will just replace the points. This can be done professionally, although re-pointing tools and spare points are available commercially for those who wish to do it themselves.

Simple darts sharpener. (Photo: WINMAU Dartboard Co. Ltd)

Darts tool kit. (Photo: WINMAU Dartboard Co. Ltd)

Finger Wax

A common sight at any match at any level in years gone by would be players rubbing chalk on the barrel of their darts to aid their grip. This action was effective but the excess chalk tended to transfer itself on to the fingers and then on to clothing. In addition, chalk residue might be transferred from the darts to the face of the dartboard, which may prompt complaints from opponents and officials.

Today, chalk is still a popular solution for sweaty fingers or general lack of grip but now a cleaner more effective alternative is available – non-slip finger wax. When used properly this leaves no visible residue on either the dart or board.

Darts Tool Kit

Shafts and flights are usually easy to replace during a game but other problems can arise so manufacturers have tried to pre-empt all eventualities by producing a small multi-functional tool that fits snugly into a pocket or on a key ring.

One example of this type of tool (shown here) includes such features as a lock wrench for cross hole shafts (basically an aid to tightening aluminium shafts); a key to close shafts (that is to tighten standard shafts); a shaft spring fixer for use with nylon shafts that have springs, which is used to push the springs back into place;

and a soft-tip key, which is employed to tighten the points of soft-tip darts.

The kit also includes an integral bottle opener and a key ring hole so this too can be attached to your key ring.

Shaft Extractor Tool

Occasionally, a plastic or nylon shaft will break during a game or due to mishandling. When they do it is usually at the barrel-shaft connection point and it often leaves the thread of the shaft embedded in the barrel. This is extremely difficult to remove… or rather was.

An extractor tool is now available

which removes shaft and tip threads in seconds. Because of their small size these tools are most commonly marketed with a key ring.

Darts Scorers

After the cribbage board, the blackboard and chalk, pen and dry-wipe whiteboards and mechanical scorers came electronic scorers.

With these you merely set the score at, say, 501 for each player (or team). After each throw, the individual score is entered into the keyboard and with the press of a button the score is instantly deducted and the remaining total displayed. More sophisticated versions offer additional features, including the ability to recover all previous scores and the production of players' and teams' averages.

Electronic scorers are all well and good but in a pub or club manual scoring (for example, scoreboard and chalk) is still the favourite as it encourages more social interaction between players. This also

remains the best way for a novice player to learn the art of scoring, which involves not only subtraction but also multiplication and addition.

With soft-tip or electronic darts (a few examples of which can be found in Britain), so popular in parts of Europe and the USA, all such features, and so much more, are built in. The score from each dart is recorded, shown automatically and then stored in the machine's memory. So where soft-tip darts is organized into local, provincial or regional leagues, results can be fed instantly into a central computer database so, within a very short space of time, results and league positions are known to all, together with each player or teams' averages. This information will probably be available even before players have packed their darts away after a match and are preparing to go home.

Ear Plugs

Believe it or not, some professional players have been so distracted by

crowd noise of late they have resorted to using ear plugs to reduce the cacophony of sound and help them concentrate.

This may not be a problem for those playing at a local or league level but this accessory is included here because the one thing I do not want to happen is for any novice player to be put off the great sport of darts merely because of the sound emanating from those watching them play. If ear plugs aid concentration and help improve your performance, then use them.

As far as I am aware, no darts company has yet ventured into independent ear plug manufacturing so, if you believe ear plugs can help you, you can pick up a pack at a very reasonable price on your next visit to Boots or Superdrug.

Wristbands

At first it might seem a little unusual that wristbands should be manufactured for participants in a sport

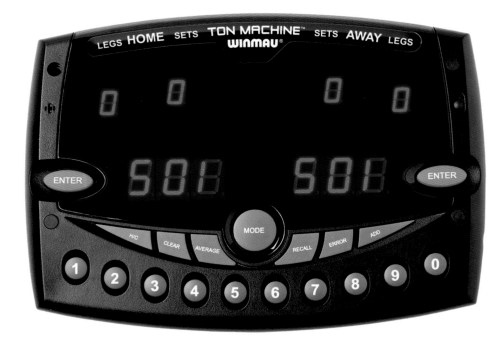

An example of an electronic scorer. (Photo: WINMAU Dartboard Co. Ltd)

An example of a personalized dartboard. (Photo: WINMAU Dartboard Co. Ltd)

that appears to be fairly static. However, many darts matches, especially under intense lighting, cause players to require something to keep them cool and dry to ensure their continuing good performance. For such occasions, stylish and functional sports elasticated wristbands (usually bearing a company logo) made of ultra-absorbent fabric are available.

Personalized Accessories

There usually comes a time in the life of most players when they at least consider investing in personalized accessories. Many will stop short and just carry on playing as usual with their normal darts and accessories but increasing numbers of players, especially those who are becoming successful at whatever level, want a little more; something that identifies them as an individual.

Such products range from flights, darts and shafts with your name or nickname on to darts cases embossed with your identifying logo, personalized dartboards and surrounds and clothing.

Most darts manufacturers cater for this and a look at their catalogues will show you the entire range of products available that can be personalized to your specific needs.

Whether any of this 'personalization' will make you play better darts is debatable but if it helps instil self-confidence, which in turn improves your darting skills, then the investment must be considered worthwhile.

CHAPTER 10

OTHER GAMES TO PLAY ON A DARTBOARD

Over and above the -01 games and those described in Chapter 7 there are many games that can be played on a standard dartboard, including some based on other recognized sports.

In this chapter, you will be introduced to a number of those alternative games, ones that not only help to improve your play but also add an element of fun to your practice routine. They can also be played at your pub, club or academy with your darting friends.

There have been some immensely complicated alternative games that can be played on the dartboard, one of the most complicated being Jumbo Landing. This was the invention of darts player Steve Watton in the 1980s and used darts to land a jumbo jet on the kitchen table (thankfully not literally), where the dartboard was the 'control panel' and the darts were the 'flying instructions'.

Fortunately, for the less complex examples in this chapter, all you need are your darts, a dartboard, an ordinary scoreboard and, of course, opponents.

I begin with three traditional sports that have been transferred to the dartboard, namely bowls, cricket and football but, rest assured, you do not have to have played or understood these in order to enjoy playing them on a dartboard.

Bowls

Bowls is a sport in which wooden balls are rolled down a manicured lawn (or along a mat in the case of the indoor version) called the rink at a small white round ball called the jack, which is situated at the far end of the rink. The aim is to roll your bowl as close as possible to the jack or, better still, come into contact with it. Points are allocated in accordance with whose bowl or bowls are nearest to the jack at the end of each game, called an 'end'.

This game is easily transferred to a dartboard.

In the darts version, the bullseye represents the jack. In the actual game of bowls, bowlers take it in turns but in darts bowls individual players throw their three darts, then the next player throws theirs to see who can throw nearest the jack and score up to a maximum of three points per turn.

The game is unlikely to end well for some dart flights if too many people play darts bowls. As a team game with accurate players participating, the area around the jack/bullseye would become very crowded. This would inevitably lead to damage to darts already in the board caused by incoming darts. So it is best to play darts bowls with up to four individual players or two teams of two.

The aim of the game is for an individual or team to achieve a given target points score, say ten points. As in the real game of bowls, where a player is awarded a point or points by being the closest to the jack, so it is in the darts version. For example, if a game is being played by four individuals and one player hits a bullseye and two outer bulls and the other three players' darts all land outside of that area, then that player is awarded the maximum tally of three points.

However, in this example, if an individual player has hit a bullseye and two outer bulls and then an opponent hits an outer bull, only the dart in the bullseye will score and give the player only one point. In the event that another player also hits the bullseye, then this end is halved or, in some games, called a draw with either no point or half a point being awarded to either player.

As the jack in a proper game of bowls is never in the same place, although it is always in the same line, darts players can vary their version by moving the jack up or down from the bullseye, declaring that (up the board) treble 20 or double 20 represents the jack or (moving down the dartboard) treble 3 or double 3 is the target.

While the standard game of darts bowls can improve accuracy on the bullseye, this variation clearly has the same benefit to those wishing to become more consistent on these other selected doubles and trebles.

Cricket

In summer the sound of willow thwacking against leather resonates around many a village green and out of your television. In both cases, the teams of eleven men or women aim to bowl out their opponents in the shortest possible time and for the smallest score within a given timescale. Each player out is a wicket and the scores obtained are known as runs.

As with darts bowls, English cricket translates easily on to the standard dartboard.

Whereas the number of players in darts bowls needs, because of the very nature of the game, to be restricted, darts cricket is best played as a team game. Provided each of the two teams competing have the same number of players, in heory it does not matter what size he teams are. However, being sensible, very large teams can become unwieldy so I would suggest they are restricted to a maximum of four players per side.

Once the teams have been decided by mutual discussion or perhaps throwing nearest the bullseye – in a four-handed game the two nearest the bullseye play the two furthest away – each team elects a team captain and players then spend a few minutes deciding what their team should be called. (The latter is not compulsory. Often just writing the players' initials along the top of the scoreboard will suffice.)

Which team will throw (or rather bowl) first is usually determined by the two opposing captains throwing one dart at the bullseye (also known as bulling up), the nearest then deciding whether their team will 'bat' or 'bowl'.

Once these formalities have been completed, the name of the team batting first is written on the scoreboard along with its ten intact wickets. This is how it would look:

BOB'S XI

The team that is bowling throws first, followed by the opponent's first batsman. The bowler throws three darts at the bullseye (the wicket). If he or she hits the outer bull, they score one wicket. Hitting the bullseye scores two wickets. As each wicket is lost, the wickets shown on the scoreboard are reduced accordingly.

After each bowler has thrown their three darts, provided there is at least one wicket left standing, a member of the batting team throws, the purpose being to score as many points as possible with their three darts, their

runs then being credited to the team by way of a running total on the scoreboard.

However, in darts cricket, only points scored in excess of 40 are counted as runs. So, if a player hits treble 20 (60 points), a single 13 and a single 2, the total score is 75 but the runs awarded are 35. Bowlers and those batting throw alternately until all ten wickets have been lost. But before that, let's see how Bob's XI is doing after a few throws.

BOB'S XI

| | | |

63

It looks as though Bob's team is making hard work of it as it has lost six of its original ten wickets for only 63 runs. Clearly Captain Bob will be hoping the lower order will improve things! In fact, in this example they do and are eventually all out for 143. (As in ordinary cricket, if one team is hitting huge scores the captain can decide to declare in order to give the opposing side a chance.)

At the end of Bob's team's innings, its score is recorded at the top of the scoreboard, so at the start of the opponent's innings the scoreboard looks like this:

Bob's XI – 143 all out

COLIN'S CREW

| | | | |

| | | | |

The roles are reversed with Colin's team becoming the batting side and Bob's the bowlers. The game is then played out to the end, with Bob's team having to bowl out Colin's Crew before it can exceed the score of 143, in which case

victory is Bob's. However, if Bob's XI fails to bowl Colin's Crew out and the opponents exceed 143 then his team will be beaten.

As in the proper game of cricket, drawn games are also possible in the darts version. On most occasions, these are automatically accepted but, if a winner has to be determined for whatever reason, then an extra eleventh wicket can be played in order to determine the winner.

In some variations of the rules of darts cricket, inaccuracy is punished. For example, in the case of the team that is bowling, if a bowler when aiming for the bullseye/outer bull throws his or her dart outside the treble ring, then whatever that errant dart scores is credited to the batting side.

If any of the batting side throws a dart that lands outside of the scoring area of the dartboard (known in darts slang as being 'off the island') then they are deemed to have run themselves out and the team loses a wicket. Also, if a player on the batting side accidentally hits the bullseye or outer bull then they lose two wickets or one wicket respectively.

One major benefit of the darts version of cricket has over the proper game is that it can never be a case of 'rain stops play'!

Football

One of Britain's great national pastimes and the most popular of English sports that has now infatuated the entire planet, football, like bowls and cricket, is transferable easily to the dartboard. It is simple to learn and is a fascinating and competitive game for two players or, more appropriately, two teams. It is a game that rewards accuracy and punishes inaccuracy.

The first team to ten goals or the team that has scored the most goals in a given time limit is the winner. In the latter version of the game, a draw is possible, just like the real thing.

Teams (of equal numbers of players) are decided among the players themselves or, if that is not possible, the sides can be determined by each player throwing one dart at the bullseye. For example, where there are eight players, the four nearest the bullseye might play the four furthest from the centre. Captains of each side are then agreed.

The next stage is to come up with team names, just to add a little authenticity to the game. The order of play is determined by the two captains either bulling up or simply tossing a coin. The team winning the bull-up or the toss has possession of the 'ball', this being the bullseye.

While a team has possession of the ball, the players in that team throw for doubles. Any double will do. Each double hit constitutes one goal, so a player has the opportunity to score three goals per turn. That team scores as many goals as it can, each goal being recorded on the scoreboard, before the opposing side gains possession of the ball by hitting a bullseye, at which point the roles are reversed.

As individual team players throw alternately, the ball may be in one team's possession only briefly as the opponents only have to hit a bullseye to achieve a successful tackle. Once having gained possession, the other team goes for doubles (goals) until it is tackled. If dispossessed by the opponent hitting a bullseye (or in more casual games the outer bull counts as the ball too) the game continues, tackle after tackle, goal after goal until one team achieves the target of ten goals or time runs out, in which case the team leading at that time takes the glory. A darts football match in progress might look like this on the scoreboard:

ROVERS UNITED

7   6

If during the game any player in possession of the ball hits a bullseye

accidentally (and they would have to be terrible at darts to achieve this) this is considered to be a bad pass, the opposition then taking possession. Indeed, in some versions of the game, hitting the bullseye (or outer bull) while in possession of the ball is deemed to be an own goal. A goal is then awarded to your opponent while that side retains the ball.

This game is great fun but also has a serious side as it affords the players essential practice on doubles (*any* double) and the bullseye.

****

Over and above games derived from other sports, there are other alternative darting diversions that you will enjoy and, as always, there are no difficult or detailed rules to learn.

Noughts and Crosses

Gone are the days when the simple game of noughts and crosses could be found chalked on walls or pavements, a time when children eagerly grabbed paper and crayon and amused themselves in the company of friends. Nowadays, computer games have more or less taken over completely and the simplicity of noughts and crosses (or tic-tac-toe as it is called in the United States) has been lost on them and, one might have thought, been lost in time too.

Not so the darts version.

As you will be aware the purpose of the game of noughts and crosses is to be the first to achieve a straight line, down, across or diagonally, of either three noughts or three crosses, each player taking it in turns to place a nought or a cross. Here is a completed game:

X	0	0
X	X	X
0		0

The person with the 'X' has won on this occasion.

In the darts version, the aim is similar but instead of writing 'O' or 'X' in the chosen boxes, the nine boxes are drawn on the scoreboard and the numbers one to nine written up thus:

1	2	3
4	5	6
7	8	9

Players then throw three darts in turn to try to hit the corresponding numbers (single, double or treble, they all count) on the dartboard. If they achieve that then either an 'O' or an 'X' (depending on who has been allocated them) replaces that number on the scoreboard.

After a couple of throws, the grid might look like this:

X	2	0
X	0	6
X	8	0

'X' has won the game again.

But in this beginner's version, like the original paper and crayon version of noughts and crosses, the game can be over much too soon to have been of any benefit to either player. Thus the way in which most darts players engage in the game of noughts and crosses is to shoot for the double of the numbers.

This too can become boring; a grid

of nine numbers always having the potential for stalemate. So to attempt to reduce the chances of this happening and to spice up the game, the nine numbers on the grid are determined at random by the players. In this event the nine-square matrix might look like this at the beginning of the game:

1	14	7
19	50	9
12	3	6

In this case '50' represents the bullseye.

After a few throws the grid might look like this:

X	14	7
0	0	9
X	3	6

'O' is in the best position at the moment but things can change at the throw of a dart. There are still opportunities for 'X' to win but he might have to block the '9' first.

The nine-box matrix may still lead to stalemate when good players are playing against each other so, to overcome this possibility the grid can be extended to sixteen thus:

1	2	3	4
5	6	7	8
9	10	11	1
13	14	15	6	⑰

Players now throw in turn, trying to hit the doubles (or, if you prefer, trebles) of these numbers. The aim is still to achieve 'three in a row' either horizontally, vertically or diagonally. In my experience

this version is best played by two teams of two.

Let's say that Hilary and Peter (HP) are playing Roger and Maureen (RM). The game is under way and after a few throws each the position is this:

1	2	HP	4
RM	HP	7	RM
9	10	HP	RM
13	14	RM	16	⑰

Both teams are in a good position to win, Hilary and Peter needing double 9, double 7 or double 16 while Roger and Maureen can win by hitting double 4 or double 16. As both teams can win on the latter, then double 16 would seem the best target for both sides. After another couple of throws, Roger and Maureen (RM) hit double 16 to secure the win; the final grid looking like this:

1	2	HP	4
RM	HP	7	RM
9	10	HP	RM
HP	14	RM	RM	⑰

The initials are then rubbed off of the scoreboard, leaving those numbers that were not hit in place.

If the teams are to continue playing the number 17 shown at the side of the scoreboard indicates the next number to start with to complete the new grid, which at the beginning of the next round will look like this:

1	2	17	4
18	19	7	20
9	10	Bull	1
2	14	3	4	⑤

The game then restarts with this revised matrix. Note that the number 5 is now written to the right of the scoreboard, that being the next number to use should there be a third game.

The sixteen-number grid version of noughts and crosses happens to be my favourite alternative darts game as, apart from being very competitive and great fun, it gives you practice on doubles, teaches you how to play as a team member and also makes you think tactically in terms of where you go next to try to achieve three-in-a-row and win the game.

Beat the Score

The aim of this game is given away in the title. You simply have to beat the score a player has left you but time is limited as each player is only allowed five 'lives'.

Once the order of play has been decided, usually by bulling up, the players' names are written on the scoreboard in the order they were nearest the bullseye, with their five lives against them thus:

Barry	I I I I I
Denise	I I I I I
Carole	I I I I I
Jim	I I I I I
Charlie	I I I I I

The player whose name is at the bottom of the list, in this example Charlie, must throw three darts at the dartboard with his non-throwing hand (left hand if right-handed, right hand if left-handed). The total of Charlie's scoring darts (sometimes when throwing with your wrong hand a player will miss the board completely) is the score that Barry, at the top of the list, must beat: not equal, beat.

In this example, Barry beats the score, his turn is over and all his lives are intact. The next player, Denise, has to then beat the score Barry left. She throws her three darts and scores less than the target score, so loses one life; one life being wiped off or struck through on the scoreboard.

Denise throws again, and again fails to beat Barry's score. Another life is lost. But on the third attempt she beats the score, and thus the score she leaves has to be beaten by the next player, Carole. Unfortunately Carole is playing particularly badly that day and is unable to beat Denise's score, thereby losing all her five lives. She will now sit out the rest of the game. This leaves Jim to beat Carole's score which, in this example, he does but loses three lives in the process.

Then it is Charlie's turn to try to beat the score left by Jim. He loses one life in the process and leaves the score that Barry has to beat. So, at the end of this first round, the scoreboard looks like this:

Barry	I I I I I
Denise	I I I I
Carole	
Jim	I I
Charlie	I I I I

The game continues in this way until four out of the five players in this example have run out of lives; the last man (or woman) standing with lives or a life remaining is the winner.

****

As already mentioned, the alternative games shown here are only a fraction of those that can be played on a dartboard, all of which are competitive, enjoyable and help to improve both your darting and social skills. I sincerely hope your own game benefits from these alternatives.

Finally, just for fun…

Hit the Fiver

When I was young, this game was called Hit the Ten Bob Note (an old ten shilling note), then that was withdrawn and replaced by a 50p piece so the name was changed to Hit the Quid (a £1 note). That too was consigned to history so the game became Hit the Fiver.

All you need in addition to your darts and a dartboard is a £5 note. This is opened out and pinned flat against the dartboard so the centre of the fiver is directly over the bullseye.

The aim is to hit the note with three consecutive darts (one throw). Sounds easy? Surely any reasonably proficient darts player can hit a £5 note three times

out of three throwing from the standard oche?

Ah, but it is not so easy when you learn each dart must be thrown from a different distance.

The first dart must be thrown from the standard throw line. For the second shot, the player must take one step forward of the oche and throw from there. For the third shot, the player must return to the oche and then take a step *back* and throw from that position. (In some cases the forward and back throw lines are agreed and chalked on the floor or carpet.)

The first player to place all three of his or her darts in the £5 note in one throw of three darts is declared the winner.

Although this game is always played for fun, it can be spiced up a little by each player putting £1 in the pot: the minimum number of players being five, the maximum being as many as wish to participate. The playing order is decided by bulling up, the player nearest the bull starting first, the second nearest second and so on. The first player to land his or her three darts out of three from those three positions (regardless of how many players are still waiting to throw) wins the £5 note.

You'll enjoy this game. I promise.

However, given the rapidity of notes being converted into coins, perhaps this game should be permanently renamed Hit the Banknote.

CHAPTER 11

REGIONAL DARTBOARDS

Contrary to popular belief the standard, trebles dartboard does not rule all the oches in the United Kingdom.

When the National Darts Association (NDA), based in London, declared the trebles board as standard in the 1920s, that ruling was soon accepted by players and leagues in the south and south-east but met tough resistance elsewhere, especially in the Midlands and north of England. This might explain why pockets of resistance exist in some parts of the country even today.

The purpose of this chapter is to alert you to the possibility in your travels of coming across examples of what have come to be known as regional dartboards. While a number of regional dartboards extant in the 1920s have fallen by the wayside, there are four that still flourish and have their own leagues and organizers.

These are the London Fives (wide and narrow), the Yorkshire, the Burton (also known as the Staffordshire) and the stand alone Manchester (Log End) boards. In this chapter you will also be made aware of the Quadro dartboard, which is not a regional board as such but a modern 1990s development occasionally found in pubs and clubs.

London Fives

Originating in the capital in the late Victorian period, the London Fives board is the natural extension of the miniature archery target that early darts players found too easy to hit.

The design of the earliest Fives board was of twelve segments in three sequences of, from the top of the dartboard in a clockwise direction, 20, 5, 15, 10 (see image) with a bullseye, an outer bull and a doubles ring. The twelve segments explains why the Fives board was also known as the Clock board. The modern example, shown here, includes the treble ring.

The board is traditionally hung at 5ft 6in, with the oche set at 9ft.

The game played on the Fives board was 121 Holes. Each player scored 1 point for each 5 scored with three darts. For example, if a player hit a single 20 with his or her first dart, a treble 15 with their second and double 10 with their third, their total score for that round would be 15 points (20 + 45 + 20 = 85 divided by 5 = 17).

Scored on a cribbage board (thus 121 rather than 120), the game could only be finished on the exact number, so the 'bust' rule (see Chapter 5) applied if the actual number required was exceeded.

There are two slightly different Fives boards, the Wide Fives and the Narrow Fives. Self-explanatory, the doubles (and later the trebles) were, theoretically, much easier to hit on the Wide Fives board (sometimes unkindly called the Ladies board) than the smaller segments on the Narrow Fives.

The treble ring was added to the Fives board in the 1920s in response to the growing popularity of the standard board. This made the total of 121 easily achievable, so the game was changed to 305-up and, for team play, 705-up and 1,005-up.

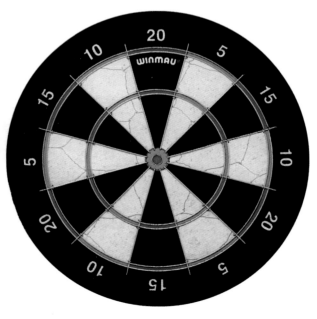

The London Narrow Fives board. (Photo: WINMAU Dartboard Co. Ltd)

The Yorkshire board, forerunner of the standard, trebles dartboard. (Photo: WINMAU Dartboard Co. Ltd)

The Fives board is still to be found in a number of London pubs, particularly in East London, and at the time of writing Fives is still played in some areas of Suffolk, including Ipswich.

It was this dartboard that eventually led to the creation of what has become known as the standard dartboard. However, the development had another stage to go through before that board was reached.

Yorkshire Board

The Yorkshire board is, sequentially, the 'father' of the standard dartboard. It has twenty segments and is numbered in the familiar way but has neither the treble ring nor outer bull.

Research has shown the original Yorkshire board was fashioned by a Yorkshireman, Thomas Buckle, from a London Fives board in the early part of the twentieth century. Buckle extended the Fives board to twenty segments, numbered 1 to 20 in random order. Standard -01 games were usually played on the Yorkshire board, as was Slip-up (see later in this chapter).

The numbering is what we know today as 'standard', suggesting that *all* regional dartboards featuring that sequence, such as the Lincoln and Black Irish, were derived from Buckle's dartboard.

It was the 'southerners' who added the treble ring a little later, thus, for the only time in any target game, moving the highest scoring segment away from the bullseye. Indeed, all darts players would do well to seek out the Yorkshire dartboard (the board is still thriving in parts of the county) to

see how the game was played originally without trebles or the outer bull.

Kent Doubles Board

The Kent Doubles board is of standard size and numbering, and was made originally of elm (now normally bristle). This board has no treble ring and only an inner bullseye. So far this description matches that of the Yorkshire board described above but there the similarities end. The Kent Doubles board is traditionally dyed black but what sets this board apart from the rest is that the scoring area extends fully to the outer edge of the dartboard; the 1 to 20 numbering having to be written or stencilled on the wall or the cabinet surround.

There are a number of Kent Doubles leagues still extant in the Garden of England.

Burton (or Staffordshire) Board

The Burton board shares the same number of segments and the same sequence of numbers as the Yorkshire board and at first sight looks identical except that, when you look closer, you will notice two boxes outside the accepted scoring area between, on the left-hand

The Kent Doubles board, rarely seen today is shown here in 1973. (Photo: Darts World/PC Archive)

The Burton (or Staffordshire) board is still occasionally found today. (Photo: Author's Darts Archive)

side, the number 14 and the number 9 and, on the right-hand side, the numbers 13 and 4.

Measuring one inch square, each box scores the equivalent of the outer bull (25 points).

The other difference, unidentifiable from a photograph, is that the material used to construct the Burton dartboard was not wood but clay, Burton-on-Trent being near the area of Staffordshire known as The Potteries, where natural clay was more plentiful than poplar or elm. At the end of each game or match, the dartboard would be taken down and the holes made by the darts repaired using a little additional clay and a small roller.

At the time of writing, a small number of leagues playing on this board are known to exist in the Burton area.

Manchester (or Log End) Board

This dartboard has resisted all attempts from other regional targets to oust it from its long-established position of popularity in some areas of the city. The unique Manchester board (also called the Log End as that was what it was made from) has stayed firm and still thrives today.

The Manchester board has a playing surface of only 10in (much smaller than

any other dartboard) and, although having twenty segments, only one of the numbers (19) is in the same position as it is on the standard board. The numbering sequence starts with 4 at the top and then, moving clockwise, reads 20, 1, 16, 6, 17, 8, 12, 9, 14, 5, 19, 2, 15, 3, 18, 7, 11, 10 and 13. The Manchester board is coloured black and has an outer bull but no treble ring. Being made of wood, the board needs to be soaked overnight otherwise it will dry and crack.

In addition, the height of the dartboard from the centre of the bullseye to the floor is only 5ft 3in (5in lower than

'standard') and the length of the oche is split for gender: men throwing from a distance of 7ft 6in while women throw from 7ft 3in.

Another difference is that the -01 games are rarely played on the Manchester board. The traditional game for the Log-End is called Slip-up, where players try to go around the board, in sequence from the number 1 to number 20, then hit a specified 'returning' double and then the bullseye (outer or inner counts) to win.

The rules of Slip-up allow for shortcuts for hitting any doubles of the numbers between 1 and 10. For example, double 1 moves the player on to 3; double 2 would take the player on to 5 and double 3 on to 7 and so on. The 'returning double' will be the first double hit by either player.

One leg of Slip-up can be completed by the experts in only seven darts!

The Manchester/Log End dartboard has its own organizing body, the Manchester Log-End Dart Board Federation, details of which can be found in Useful Contacts towards the end of this book.

Quadro 240 Dartboard

The Quadro 240 dartboard is not a regional board but it is one the travelling player may come across.

The Manchester (or Log End) Board. Photo: John Gwynne)

Introduced in 1992 by Harrow Darts Technology, the word 'quadro' referred to the fact this board, although using the standard board as its starting point, had an extra ring between the double ring and the outer bull that counted four times the value of each segment. Thus, the highest score achievable on this board with one dart is 80 (as opposed to 60 on a standard dartboard) and with three darts 240 (instead of 180).

Although the Quadro was used in some major competitions in the early 1990s, even the professional players had problems working out the new three-dart finishes; the board generating many more possible combinations than they were used to. In addition, the best finish in three darts on the standard dartboard is 170 (treble 20, treble 20, bull) whereas with the Quadro it became 210 (quadruple 20, quadruple 20, bull).

This dartboard is mentioned because, although manufacture of it ceased in 2000, it can still be found occasionally in pubs around the country.

publicity purposes. In January 2013, the board was put to the test at the Lakeside World Professional Darts Championship tournament at Frimley Green, Surrey.

The Quadro 240 dartboard originally produced by Harrows Darts in 1999 caused both sensation and confusion by its introduction of a quadruple ring. (Photo: Harrows Darts)

Although it is highly unlikely you will come across the Optimal Dartboard in your travels, it has to be worth recording here how amazing it is that a

The Optimal Dartboard

For ninety years Thomas Buckle's devious numbering system was memorized and played by millions of darts players, no one giving much thought to whether or not the sequence was perfect *mathematically*. As we have already learned, the Quadro 240 Board took the sport by surprise by the inclusion of the quadruple segment. However, even that was small beer when a professor of mathematics applied his brain to reviewing the order of numbering and published the results of his research in the academic journal *Mathematics Today*.

As a result of the professor's deliberations and calculations, the board was renumbered (see photograph) but only in the lab: not permanently. This new dartboard was dubbed The Optimal Dartboard.

As soon as the research was published, the WINMAU Dartboard Company Ltd, produced the Optimal Dartboard in very limited numbers, mainly for promotional/

The 'Optimal' dartboard, which renumbers the twenty segments to correspond with the sequence determined by university mathematicians. (Photo: WINMAU Dartboard Co. Ltd)

professional mathematician can take time out to look into the numbering of the standard dartboard. Well done to him. His board is designed to remove the perceived bias towards the beginner by ensuring that the segments run odd-even-odd-even, whereas the standard dartboard has groups of odd and even numbers together, which helps anyone new to the game. The sequence of numbers was also amended in accordance with the professor's formulae, presenting the player with a totally 'new' board.

The Optimal Dartboard did not find favour with darts players and it prompted professional darts player Bobby George to comment: 'It's a Mickey Mouse gimmick. It's the same board and same numbers but in different places; not much difference counting-wise.' However, Ian Flack, sales and marketing director of WINMAU, said: 'It was great to transfer the professor's ideas from paper to dartboard. Our especially adapted WINMAU Blade 4 dartboard went down well at Lakeside and has generated a lot of interest elsewhere.'

Never produced commercially, the Optimal Dartboard is included here to indicate the development of new ideas in relation to the dartboard continue and that even leading

The Bingo Dartboard. (Photo: Author's Darts Archive)

academics are fascinated by our sport!

Other Dartboards

Over the years, the dartboard industry has attempted to vary the dart players' experience by manufacturing boards based on other sports or games. Since the 1930s, these have included football, shove ha'penny, card games, golf and, one of the most popular, snooker and, probably the most complicated, bingo.

Although some of these variations have held dart players' attention for a short while, the majority soon go back to their favourite board, be it the standard or one of the few remaining regional targets.

GLOSSARY

Against the darts – If the player who started second in a game wins then he or she is said to have won the game 'against the darts'.

An awkward lie – A player's view of his or her intended target, for example treble 20, is obscured by a preceding dart or darts. In such cases it is usually necessary for the player to either move along the oche to gain a better view or to opt for a **cover shot** (q.v.).

Arrows – A slang term for darts, hinting at a possible historic link with archery.

Barrel – The main body of the dart, made primarily today from tungsten alloy but formerly of brass or wooden construction.

BDO – The British Darts Organisation was established in 1973 and was responsible for transforming the game into a national sport during the 1970s and 1980s and greatly increasing its presence on television. The organization's mission statement is 'Darts for all', which summarizes succinctly the BDO's present purpose.

Bed – This refers to any scoring segment of the dartboard, for example 'the 20 bed'.

Bed and breakfast – This relates to the score of 26, usually comprising, single 20, single 5 and single 1. This was originally based on the price of B & B around the onset of the twentieth century when bed and breakfast cost two shillings and sixpence (2s 6d) or 'two and six', thus 26.

Belophilite – A word created in 1988 by The Queen's English Society at the request of the author meaning 'darts player'. However, this has rarely, if ever, been used presumably because 'belo' sounds very close to 'belly'.

Bling – Incredibly loud and gaudy jewellery worn by some players, especially at exhibitions. Extreme example: England's Bobby George.

Bogey number – Those scores under 170 that is it impossible to finish in three darts, namely, in descending order, 169, 168, 166, 165, 163, 162 and 159. The only 'bogey number' under 100 that cannot be finished in two darts is 99.

Bounce out – A thrown dart hits the wire of a segment or a dart already in the board and bounces out. This can also happen with dartboards in poor condition.

Bullseye – The inner centre circle of the dartboard that scores 50 points but also counts as double 25.

Bulling up – In most games, who throws first is determined by each player throwing one dart at the bullseye; the nearest starting the game. This is known as 'bulling-up' and is also often called 'Middle for Diddle'.

Bust – If, towards the end of a game, you hit more than the total you require then you have **bust** (or 'burst') your score and on your next throw revert to the original number you had been going for. However, players need to be aware of the **No bust** rule (q.v.).

Caller – The player or official designated at a match to call out the players' individual scores so they can be recorded by the **Chalker** (q.v.). Often the calling is undertaken by a referee.

Chalker – The traditional name for the person who scores a game of darts using chalk and a blackboard. Other terms include 'scribe' or 'marker'.

Clickety-click – 66. One of many examples of 'bingo lingo' that has found its way into the language of darts over the past century or so.

Cover shot – Where a player's intended target (for example, treble 20) has been obscured by an earlier dart, one of the options is to change tack and go for a cover shot, an alternative treble, in this case usually the next highest treble, treble 19.

Dartboard – The target used in the game of darts. The standard is the trebles board but across the UK you may well stumble upon regional variations including the Fives, the Yorkshire or the Manchester boards.

Dartitis – This can be compared to the 'yips' in golf where the golfer is unable to follow through. The Oxford English Dictionary defines dartitis as: 'A state of nervousness which prevents a player from releasing a dart at the right moment when throwing.'

Darts – The three small metal projectiles used in the game of darts.

Double – The outer ring of a standard dartboard that scores twice the value of the segment.

Double in – This refers to a match where players have to hit any double before they can start to score. This method of beginning a game is a lot less common than it once was but it is still used in some leagues and competitions. Today most games are **straight in** (*q.v.*).

Double out – In all standard -01 games a double is required to finish. The double must reduce the player's score to exactly zero.

Double top – Double 20, also known as Top of the House or Top of the Shop.

Double trouble – A player is having great difficulty hitting his or her starting or finishing double(s).

Downstairs – The area at the bottom of the dartboard, double 3 and the doubles immediately on either side.

Exhibition – The opportunity for players to relax and meet the fans. A show featuring one or more top professional and exhibition players that consists primarily of the player(s) taking on a number of fans in a single game of 501-up or 701-up. Players also demonstrate trick shots and include a Q & A session at the end of the evening.

Feathers – 33. This expression is rarely heard these days but was once very popular, especially in and around London. It derives from the Cockney expression 'firty-free fousand feathers on a frushe's froat'. Where that expression has its origins is, apparently, lost in the mists of time.

Flight – Made of cardboard or polypropylene, this helps stabilize the darts once thrown.

Game On! – In most darts matches that include a caller or referee, this is usually uttered by the official to notify both the players and the audience the match is under way. In a noisy match environment this may be preceded by a request that those present give the players the 'best of order'.

Gameshot – The shot that completes the game. The winning combination of one, two or three darts that reduces the total points to zero, finishing on the required double.

Gamesmanship – Possibly better known as 'cheating' where an opponent uses dastardly ploys such as standing behind their opponent on the oche and clicking their darts, clearing their throat and moving about within the other player's eye line in order to gain an advantage.

Highest out-shot – 170. This is the highest outshot on a standard dartboard and can only be achieved by hitting treble 20 with your first two darts (120 points), finishing with the bullseye (50 points – double 25).

House darts – Most pubs and clubs that have a dartboard also provide darts for customers to play with either free of charge or for a small donation to charity. These are usually of poor quality so, wherever possible, bring your own.

House rules – Wherever you travel with your darts, you will probably find the standard rules apply. However, this is not always the case, so always check first before you take on the locals as they may play the **no bust** (*q.v.*) rule.

Leg – One game in a match. For example, a match may be the best of seven legs; the first player to win four legs wins the match.

Madhouse – Double 1. So named because once you have reached it there is nowhere else to go!

Maximum – A score of 180 points with three darts (three treble 20s) on a standard dartboard.

Mugs away! – The player who lost the last game starts the next; the expression originating from the days when the loser always bought the winner a mug of beer.

Nine-darter – The darts player's Nirvana. The perfect game of 501 completed in nine darts, the minimum number possible to achieve that score. There are many permutations possible to achieve this.

No bust – Under some pub and club rules **no bust** is played. This rule means if a player is going for a number to finish a game or match and he or she exceeds the number required, they do not (as you would do in a standard game) **bust** (*q.v.*) the score and go back to where they started on their next throw. With no bust only the one or two scoring darts are counted, that is only the darts they scored with before they bust.

Oche – Also known as the 'throw line' or 'toe line', this is the line behind which all players must stand in order to throw. The word was originally spelt 'hockey', after the line used in some versions of skittles but, for whatever reason, was changed to oche in the 1970s by the BDO.

Off the island – When a dart completely misses the scoring area of the dartboard it is described as being 'off the island'.

Outer bull – The outer ring around the bullseye that scores 25 points. It is also simply known as 'the 25'.

Out-shot – The number required to complete a game in three darts or fewer. It is also called the 'checkout'.

PDC – The Professional Darts Corporation (PDC) is the organization created in 1993 (originally called the World Darts Council) that serves the interests of professional players at home and worldwide.

Perfect game – This occurs when a player achieves the best possible finish; for example, a game of 101 in two darts, 301 in six darts, 501 in nine darts or 1,001 in seventeen darts.

Professional darts player – Any player who makes his or her living entirely from darts or for whom darts is their main source of income.

Rankings – Players in the professional game work hard to achieve the highest possible space on the ranking table or, in the case of the Professional Darts Corporation (PDC), the Order of Merit. Ranking tables are usually determined by the accumulation of ranking points won at ranking events around the country, Europe and even the rest of the world. In the case of the PDC, the Order of Merit is determined by the amount of prize money earned.

Red bit – Although there are many scoring segments on a standard board that are coloured red, the term 'red bit' always refers to the treble 20 bed. (Also known as the 'lipstick'.)

Robin Hooding – A situation where a following dart becomes stuck in the shaft of an earlier dart in the board during one throw of three darts.

'Scoring for Show, Doubles for Dough' – This is a term coined by English professional Bobby George and means you can hit as many high scores as you like during a game but it is the winning double that earns you the money. (This is also the title of Bobby George and the author's book of 'darts lingo', which was published in 2011.)

Segment – Any of the areas on the standard board that score points: doubles, trebles, singles, outer bull and the bullseye.

Set – Where matches are decided by winning a specific number of sets, each set comprises a given number of **legs** (q.v.). For example, if a match is the best of twelve sets, the first to seven sets wins.

Shaft – Also known as the stem, this is the component part of a dart that screws into the **barrel** (q.v.) at one end and secures the **flight** (q.v.) in place. It is usually made of polypropylene or aluminium.

Shanghai – To hit a single, double and treble of the same number in consecutive darts (usually in any order) is known as shanghai. As with **three in a bed** (q.v.), in some friendly matches a player who achieves shanghai is often awarded the match.

Spider – The wires or metal framework that defines each segment of a dartboard.

Stance – The way a player stands at the oche to throw his or her darts.

Straight in – In most games of darts today there is no need, as there was some years ago, to hit a starting double before you can score in a game. Nowadays, most games are 'straight in' so only a finishing double is needed.

Suffering – A sympathetic utterance from friends or your opponent as you try unsuccessfully time and again to hit that winning double.

Take chalks (or 'To chalk') – Traditionally a player waiting for a game can write his or her initials in chalk on the scoreboard to earn the right to score (or 'chalk') the next game and play the winner of the subsequent one. The winning player stays on until he or she is beaten. Then they may chalk their initials up again and so on.

Taking the odd off – When a player has left an odd number, say, 23, 57 or 63, he or she must take the odd off, hopefully with their first dart, to leave them with an even number with which to finish the game.

Ton – A score of 100 in three darts. Any score in excess of 100 points is usually called a 'ton-plus'. Hitting 140 is called a 'ton-forty', while to score 180 (three treble 20s) is called either a 'ton-eighty' or, more commonly, a **maximum** (q.v.).

Three in a bed – To score 'three in a bed' is to land all three of your darts in the same scoring segment, be it singles, doubles, trebles, the outer bull or the bullseye. Sometimes, in friendly matches, you are awarded the game if you hit three trebles or three doubles in one throw of three darts.

To split – If a player, for example, going for double 10, misses the double completely with his or her first dart, then hits a single 10 with their second dart and then, when going for double 5 with their third dart, hits a single 5, the player's turn is ended and he or she is said to have '5 to split'. That is, they have to **take the odd off** (q.v.) on their next throw to have a chance of hitting a winning double.

Treble – The inner ring of a standard board between the double ring and the outer bull. This scores three times the value of the segment.

Tungstens – An abbreviation of tungsten darts.

Two hens – Two 10s (double 10) derived from Cockney rhyming slang, of which this is only one example.

WDF – The World Darts Federation (WDF) was formed in 1977 with the view to being the umbrella organization for darts across the globe. It currently has 69 member countries.

Wet feet! – An expression used by onlookers or an opponent to indicate a player standing at the oche has his or her feet over the throw line.

With the darts – If the player who throws first in a game wins, then that game is said to have gone 'with the darts'.

Wrong bed – A player hits the double next to the one he or she was aiming at. For example, if throwing for double 10 the player hits either double 6 or double 15 then they are said to be in the wrong bed.

If you wish to learn more about the language of darts ('darts lingo') see Further Reading.

EPILOGUE

In this book I have provided you with sound advice and guidance on the techniques and skills you need to play and enjoy the most sociable of all indoor games at the level you have chosen.

In recent years, darts has experienced a renaissance in both popularity and participation. Long may it continue to grow and, with the help of this book, encourage everyone, of any age, whether able-bodied or disabled, male or female, to take up the sport of darts.

As you step up to the oche, I wish you all well and, of course, every success. But most of all *enjoy* your darts.

GAME ON!

England's Lisa Ashton, the 2015 Lakeside Women's World Darts Champion, adds another victory to her tally. (Photo: Tip Top Pics Ltd)

Dutch star Michael van Gerwen celebrates yet another major title win. (Photo: Tip Top Pics Ltd)

USEFUL CONTACTS

Owing to the ever changing names and addresses of individuals involved with any sport, printed lists seem to go out of date so quickly. To minimize this effect, this list comprises primarily the website addresses for key organizations, examination of which should lead to the main contact e-mail address for enquiries.

Key Administrative Bodies

British Darts Organisation (BDO) – www.bdodarts.com

Professional Darts Corporation (PDC) – www.pdc.tv

Regional Bodies

England Darts Organisation – www.englanddarts.co.uk

Manchester Log End Dartboard Federation – Secretary: John Gwynne, email: johngwynne45@gmail.com

Northern Ireland Darts Organisation (NIDO) – www.northernirelanddarts.com

Irish National Darts Organisation (INDO) – www.facebook.com/pages/INDO-Darts

More information about darts in Eire can be found at www.dartsinireland.com

Scottish Darts Organisation (SDO) – www.scottishdarts.com

Welsh Darts Organisation (WDO) – www.welshdarts.com

County Darts

Many UK counties are affiliated to the British Darts Organisation. Details of those counties' contacts can be found at www.bdodarts.com (Click down list 'Counties' and then select the one(s) you want. For non-affiliated counties, I suggest you search the web for 'Darts', followed by the county you are looking for.

Local Darts

Many local darts clubs and leagues have their own websites these days. Just Google the town or city and add 'darts' and you should find something.

World Darts

World Darts Federation (WDF) – www.wdf.com.

At the time of writing, the WDF has over 65 countries affiliated to it and so details of the key contacts for each can be found here. If the country you are searching for cannot be found on the WDF website, I suggest you simply web search darts'.

Lakeside, Frimley Green, Surrey – www.lakesideworlddarts.co.uk.

This venue is regarded by many darts players and fans as The Home of World Darts, having been the venue for the BDO World Darts Championship and numerous international darts events for many years.

Darts and Dartboard Manufacturers

WINMAU Dartboard Company Ltd – www.winmau.com

NODOR International – www.nodor-darts.com

Red Dragon Darts – www.reddragondarts.com

Harrows Darts Technology – www.harrows-darts.com

Visit these websites to obtain details of current products.

Darts and Accessories Suppliers

www.a180.co.uk

www.dartscorner.co.uk

Dartitis

For further advice and guidance concerning this condition see www.patrickchaplin.com/Dartitis.htm.

Darts for the Disabled

The World Disability Darts Association – www.world-disability-darts.org

Darts Forums

Since the advent of the worldwide web, many darts forums have been developed and thrive. I use the forums occasionally. The following are merely a sample.
www.dartsnutz.net

www.doublefinish.com

www.double16.com

www.thedartsforum.co.uk

www.tsod.tv (Note: The acronym 'tsod' stands for 'The Stars of Darts'.)

Darts History

The author of this book is regarded globally as the foremost darts historian and has a website www.patrickchaplin. com that includes more than 300 pages of information relating to the history and development of the sport. The author also produces a monthly Dr. Darts' Newsletter (DDN), which is issued free to subscribers. DDN covers aspects of the sport of darts, past, present and future. Contact info@patrickchaplin.com to subscribe.

Darts Lighting

For those who wish to professionally surround their dartboard with light then the Circumluminator may be your answer.

Details can be obtained from www. nuvolux.com.

Darts Regulation Authority (DRA)

www.thedra.co.uk

A regulatory body recognized by the Professional Darts Corporation (PDC) that ensures good governance and integrity within the sport of darts.

Darts Youth Academies

There are a growing number of youth darts academies in the UK, many under the auspices of professional darts player Steve Brown. There is space to only provide details of a few here.

Andover Youth Academy – www. andoverdarts.co.uk

Angus Darts Academy (Scotland) – www. angusdartsacademy.co.uk

Calstep Darts Academy (South Wales) – www.calstepdartswales.co. uk/#!youthacademy

Future Darts Academy (North Wales) – www.future-darts.co.uk

Steve Brown Darts Academies – http:// stevebrowndartsacademies.co.uk

Academies include Bedworth (Coventry); Bristol (2); Cannock, Staffordshire; Redruth, Cornwall; Swindon and Worcester. Visit the website for a full listing.

Stockport Darts Academy – www. stockport.ac.uk/darts-academy

Exhibitions

Professional players supplement their prize money from competitions by appearing in exhibitions across the country, playing and entertaining fans for an evening. Fans love to meet their darting heroes face to face. All top professionals have a website, for example Bobby George (www. bobbygeorge.com) so simply use the web to search using the individual's name to find the link.

One website that is a one-stop shop for exhibitions is www.dartsexhibitions.co.uk.

Other Darts Accessories

Darts Shirts

www.dartsshirts.co.uk.

This website specializes in producing personalized darts shirts for players and teams.

Personalized Flights

http://www.reddragondarts.com/ flightdesigner/

The Flight Designer is a unique technology that allows anyone with access to a PC the opportunity to design their own full-colour dart flights. The key to its success is simplicity and it is easy to create your own unique flights by simply uploading pictures and adding text. No graphic design skills are required.

Players' Organizations

Independent Dart Players Association (IDPA) – http://idpa.co.uk

Professional Dart Players Association (PDPA) – www.pdpa.co.uk

Pub Darts

When travelling and looking for a pub that has a dartboard one can usually rely on word of mouth but the one general guide that may assist you in this process is the Campaign for Real Ale's (CAMRA) (www.camra.org.uk) annual publication The Good Beer Guide. Included in the short description of each establishment will be an indicator of whether or not the pub has darts or other pub games.

Electronic or Soft-Tip Darts

www.dartslive.com/uk

Although currently of limited interest to British darts players, this pay-to-play, electronic version of darts (usually played with standard darts but with tough plastic points) is gradually making ground in some major towns and cities in the UK. For where these machines are currently available, check the website shown.

FURTHER READING

While you have all you need to learn the skills to enable you to play darts well, there may be those among you who are interested in learning more about the history of the sport, the lives of some of the professional players who have graced the oches of the UK and across the world, the unique language of darts or those who wish to learn some fascinating facts about the sport that you will not find on the internet. This section is provided for such people.

History

Chaplin, Patrick. *Darts in England – A social history* (Manchester: Manchester University Press, Hardback 2009. Softback 2012.)

Peek, Dan William. *To the Point – The Story of Darts in America* (Rocheport, MO: Totem Pointe, 2001)

Waddell, Sid. *Bellies and Bullseyes: The Outrageous True Story of Darts* (London: Ebury Press, 2007)

Lives

Barrett, Tom. *Darts* (London: Pan Books, 1973)

Bristow, Eric. *The Crafty Cockney – The Autobiography* (London: Century, 2008)

Caven, Jamie and Kirby, David. *The Way Eye See the Game – The Jamie Caven Story* (Leicester: DK Darts, 2013)

George, Bobby (with Lance Hardy). *Bobby Dazzler – My Story* (London: Orion Books, 2006)

Gulliver, Trina (with Patrick Chaplin). *Golden Girl: The Autobiography of the Greatest Ever Ladies' Darts Player* (London: John Blake, 2008)

Lowe, John (with Patrick Chaplin) *Old Stoneface: The Autobiography of Britain's Greatest Darts Player* (London: John Blake, Hardback 2005, revised and updated paperback *Old Stoneface: My Autobiography,* 2009)

Language

George, Bobby and Chaplin, Dr. Patrick *Scoring for Show, Doubles for Dough – Bobby George's Darts Lingo* (Clacton-on-Sea: Apex Publishing, 2011)

Facts

Chaplin, Patrick. *180! – Fascinating Darts Facts* (Stroud: The History Press, 2012)

INDEX